A'ūdhu billāhi minash-shaitānir-rajīm.
I seek refuge in God from the accursed satan.

Bismillāhir-Rahmānir-Rahīm.
In the name of God, the Most Compassionate, the Most Merciful.

LAILATUL-QADR
THE DAY OF LIGHT

M. R. BAWA MUHAIYADDEEN (ﺭ)

FELLOWSHIP PRESS
PHILADELPHIA, PA

This volume of *Lailatul-Qadr: The Day of Light* is unabridged and comes to these pages directly from the recorded words of M. R. Bawa Muhaiyaddeen ☮. Every effort has been made to keep the purity of his words intact. Nothing has been intentionally added, subtracted, or rearranged.

Library of Congress Control Number: 2019940652
Muhaiyaddeen, M. R. Bawa.
    Lailatul-Qadr: The Day of Light/
    M. R. Bawa Muhaiyaddeen ☮.
    Philadelphia, PA: Fellowship Press, 2019
    p. cm.
    Includes index.
    Trade paperback: 978-1-943388-45-5
    Hardcover: 978-1-943388-46-2

1. Allāh. 2. Sufism. 3. Islām. 4. Lailatul-Qadr. 5. Night of Power. 6. Ramadān. 7. Hajj. 8. Prayer. 9. Charity. 10. 'Ilm. 11. Muhammad ☮. 12. Peace. 13. Qur'ān. 14. Kalimah. 15. Tauhīd. 16. God. 17. Truth. 18. Faith. I. Title.

Copyright © 2019
by Bawa Muhaiyaddeen Fellowship
5820 Overbrook Avenue, Philadelphia, Pennsylvania 19131

All rights reserved. No portion of this document
may be reproduced in any manner
without written permission from the publisher.

Printed in the United States of America
by FELLOWSHIP PRESS
Bawa Muhaiyaddeen Fellowship
First Printing

Muhammad Raheem Bawa Muhaiyaddeen ☺

Contents

When Everything Is Recorded	1
God's Explanation	7
The Day of Meeting Allāh	23
The Rays of Light	51
The State of Readiness	63
Heaven Is the Reward	77
When the Light Descends	85
It Is All Inside	91
Revelation	93
Appendix	*105*
Glossary	*109*
Index	*127*
Muhammad Raheem Bawa Muhaiyaddeen	*133*

Sūratul-Qadr

"We have indeed revealed this (Message) in
the Night of Power:
And what will explain to thee what the Night of Power is?
The Night of Power is better than a thousand months.
Therein come down the angels and the Spirit [*rūh*] by Allāh's
permission on every errand:
Peace! This until the rise of morn!"

—The Holy Qur'ān: 97

A'ūdhu billāhi minash-shaitānir-rajīm.
I seek refuge in God from the accursed satan.
Bismillāhir-Rahmānir-Rahīm.
In the name of God, the Most Compassionate, the Most Merciful.

When Everything Is Recorded
July 23, 1980

Someone asked a question about the Night of Power before the recording began.

BAWA MUHAIYADDEEN☮ *Night-power?*

QUESTION I read somewhere—

BAWA MUHAIYADDEEN☮ I do not know anything about *that*. You have to ask those people over there or Dick Tambi[1] [the *imām*].

QUESTION I don't know. I don't know, but—

BAWA MUHAIYADDEEN☮ Ah. Then ask the question.

QUESTION I've read somewhere, that on that night all the animal kingdom and all the vegetable kingdom bow down to God and that the water in the ocean turns sweet. On that night the heavens opened up and the Qur'ān was revealed in its entirety, down to the lowest heaven, and then from there Gabriel☮ decreed, revealed it, at the appropriate times, *sūrah* by *sūrah*, chapter by chapter. I was wondering if that was accurate.

---

1. Dick Tambi   Bawangal☮ affectionately called the *imām* Dick Tambi. The *imām's* first name is Dick and *tambi* means brother in Tamil. Thus, Dick Tambi becomes Brother Dick.

BAWA MUHAIYADDEEN☮ If Gabriel☮ preserved it, to whom did it come down at the appropriate times?

QUESTION It didn't say. It just said that—to Muhammad☮, I assume. The point was that it came down to the lowest heaven, to Gabriel☮ that night, and then from that night it was revealed to Muhammad☮, *sūrah* by *sūrah*, at the appropriate times.

BAWA MUHAIYADDEEN☮ Allāh's sound came and Gabriel☮ brought it at the time it came. He brought the sounds when they came to him. On the day known as Lailatul-Qadr, the Qur'ān was made complete. It was made complete and given to the Rasūl☮. The Qur'ān was finalized at that time. It was completed.

What does it mean that Gabriel☮ came and sent each revelation down one by one at the appropriate times after storing them in the seventh heaven? Who said that? Was it in the Qur'ān?

TRANSLATOR No, it was written in the book.

BAWA MUHAIYADDEEN☮ (*laughing*) If the water of the sea had been made sweet, the people would have taken it out on that day and turned it all into sugar.

QUESTION I thought that Muhammad☮ heard the *sūrahs* one at a time.

TRANSLATOR That's true.

BAWA MUHAIYADDEEN☮ Yes. The entire Qur'ān was finalized on Lailatul-Qadr. The entire Qur'ān was completed. How was that done?

QUESTION It was on that day that the first *sūrah, iqra' bismi rabbikal-ladhī khalaq,* came on the twenty-seventh day of the fast, when he was on the mountain, and when he was told to proclaim it.

BAWA MUHAIYADDEEN ☉ So that was when the Rasūl ☉ was told to proclaim it. Did each *sūrah* come through Gabriel's command or did each one come down when Allāh commanded?

TRANSLATOR Allāh's words came down through Gabriel ☉.

BAWA MUHAIYADDEEN ☉ Yes! Each *sūrah* came down at the time it was decreed. Each one came down right away at each time. Not one *sūrah* came down without Allāh's command. When you said that Gabriel ☉ brought the entire Qur'ān and preserved it in the seventh heaven and then brought it at the appropriate time—it did not happen that way.

TRANSLATOR (*laughing*) I didn't say it! That was how she asked the question!

BAWA MUHAIYADDEEN ☉ Each of the various commandments came down at the requisite time. Each time Muhammad ☉ asked Him something, God gave him the *āyah* and the *wahy*, the verse and the revelation. He said, "O Gabriel, go tell him!" That is what God said. What the book said was wrong. Everything does *tasbīh*, and everything makes requests of God. That is the truth. They are doing *tasbīh* to Allāh even now, they are doing *tasbīh* continuously. All lives do *tasbīh* to Allāh—the sun, the moon, the stars, the water.

TRANSLATOR Not only that night, but all the time.

BAWA MUHAIYADDEEN ☉ The sweetness refers to the well of the Zam-Zam. When a person's *īmān*, a person's faith, certitude, and determination, becomes correct, the sweetness of the Zam-Zam water develops within him. This [Bawa Muhaiyaddeen ☉ is pointing to his throat] is the well of the Zam-Zam, the place from which the water flows. This is the sea of which they speak. This is what will become sweet. The body is salty. The body is made of salt. Because the body is salty, the Zam-Zam will never run dry as long as he is alive.

His *'ilm*, his knowledge of the divine, will be sweet. That is the *bahrul-'ilm*, the sea of divine knowledge. The *bahrul-'ilm* will be sweet. His *'ilm* will be sweet. That is why it was said like that. The sea water does not become sweet. The rest of his body is salty, and this is the Zam-Zam well. This water will be sweet. This *rahmah* will be sweet. This is the *bahrul-'ilm*.

They just wrote that without understanding. They write things in so many ways in the books. But if you are to learn, you need to learn here.

TRANSLATOR Who is the writer that wrote this?

QUESTION I will show it to you. It is in the book that had all the *ahādīth* about what the Qur'ān said about Ramadān and (unintelligible). But that night is—I got the feeling that that particular night seems to be—very special the entire year if someone is searching.

TRANSLATOR But nobody knows what that night is.

QUESTION That's what I'm trying to find out.

A discussion ensues among the people who are there.
The recording is turned off and then on again.

TRANSLATOR (*in Tamil*) Within him there is a day that is Lailatul-Qadr. Whenever the *rahmah*, the grace, of God is born in each person, that is the Lailatul-Qadr in his own life.

BAWA MUHAIYADDEEN ☙ I cannot say.

TRANSLATOR (*laughing*) You are the one who said that! I'm not saying it. You said that before.

BAWA MUHAIYADDEEN ☙ All I know is that a *sūrah* came down

to the Rasūl ☻ when he was on Mount Hirā'. That was the day of *īmān*. Gabriel ☻ said, "O Muhammad, proclaim these words." That was the day of *īmān* when the Qur'ān was imprinted within him.

Once, twice, three times the Rasūl ☻ was held in a crushing embrace. Gabriel ☻ gripped his *qalb*, his innermost heart, in a crushing embrace three times, and told him what to say. That was the *īmān*, that was the *rahmah*, that was the *'ilm*, that was the Qur'ān, that was the record. His *qalb* was held and squeezed. Everything which came after that was recorded. That was the *tape*. He was held in that crushing embrace so that his *qalb* would record what was being said.

Lailatul-Qadr arrives when that state comes to someone, when everything that happens thereafter is recorded. That is the day the Qur'ān comes down to him. When does that occur? On the day his heart becomes beautiful and the *zīnah*, the beauty, comes into his face. That is the day the Light in his heart and the beauty in his face come into being. Lailatul-Qadr is the day in which he receives the entire Qur'ān. He records everything that comes after that.

The sounds came from Allāh to the Rasūl ☻ through Gabriel ☻. Allāh sends it to an *Insān Kāmil*, a perfected human being, so that he can then give it to his children.[2] Thus each individual *qalb* must become *Insān Kāmil*. Gabriel ☻ brought it from Allāh to the Rasūl ☻, and then Muhammad ☻ gave it to his followers in his time.

After him, came the Qutb ☻. There is a Qutb ☻, a Shaikh, an *Insān Kāmil*, for each time, to whom that *wahy* will come, to whom those words will come.

And that is what will be given to the children.

When this *īmān*, this Light known as Lailatul-Qadr comes to you—*kadir* means Light, the Light of Allāh, not letters but Light—this is what is called Lailatul-Qadr. This is what the Qur'ān means by Lailatul-Qadr. *Kadir* means Light, each sound was Light, each word was a brilliant resplendence. Each word imprinted itself within the Rasūl ☻ at that time. Then his heart was clear, and his

---

2. children   followers who are loved and cared for as his very own family

face contained the *zīnah*. Muhammad's face was clear.

After that time, this state comes through an *Insān Kāmil*—after the Rasūl ☮, it comes through an *Insān Kāmil*, a Qutb ☮, who then reveals it and tells it to his children. Those words will come to him and what is revealed from him, what can be received from him, is Lailatul-Qadr. If you have that Light within you, you will take in words of Light—that is what will be imprinted within you. This is the meaning of the *sūrah*. You have to hold on to what comes from there, otherwise the ray of Light will not descend.

A'ūdhu billāhi minash-shaitānir-rajīm.
I seek refuge in God from the accursed satan.
Bismillāhir-Rahmānir-Rahīm.
In the name of God, the Most Compassionate, the Most Merciful.

God's Explanation
July 30, 1980

Bismillāhir-Rahmānir-Rahīm.
Allāhu akbar. Allāhu akbar. Allāhu akbar.
Lā ilāha illAllāh. Lā ilāha illAllāh. Lā ilāha illAllāh.
Muhammadur-Rasūlullāh. Muhammadur-Rasūlullāh.
Muhammadur-Rasūlullāh.
Allāhu akbar. Allāhu akbar.
Lā ilāha illAllāh.
In the name of God, the Most Compassionate, the Most Merciful.
God is greater.
There is no one other than You [O God]. You are Allāh.
Muhammad is the Messenger of God.
God is greater.
There is no one other than You [O God]. You are Allāh.

Bismillāhir-Rahmānir-Rahīm.
As-salāmu 'alaikum wa rahmatullāhi wa barakātuhu.

Bismillāhir-Rahmānir-Rahīm.
Al-hamdu lillāhi Rabbil-'ālamīn.
Ar-Rahmānir-Rahīm.
Māliki yawmid-dīn.
Iyyāka nā'budu wa iyyāka nasta'īn.
Ihdinas-sirātal-mustaqīm,
sirātal-ladhīna an'amta 'alaihim,
ghairil-maghdūbi 'alaihim wa lad-dāllin.
Āmīn.

In the name of God, the Most Compassionate, the Most Merciful.
Praise be to God, the Cherisher and Sustainer of the worlds.
The Most Compassionate, the Most Merciful.
Master of the Day of Judgment.
Thee alone do we worship and only Thine aid do we seek.
Show us the straight way,
the way of those on whom Thou hast bestowed Thy grace,
those whose (portion) is not wrath, and who go not astray.

Bismillāhir-Rahmānir-Rahīm.
Qul: Huwallāhu ahad;
Allāhus-samad,
lam yalid, wa lam yūlad;
wa lam yakul-lāhu kufuwan ahad.
In the name of God, the Most Compassionate, the Most Merciful.
Say: He is God, the One and Only;
God, the Eternal, Absolute;
He begetteth not, nor is He begotten;
and there is none like unto Him.
Āmīn.

Bismillāhir-Rahmānir-Rahīm.
Allāh!
The One who created us
to go on the straight path is Allāh!
The One who gave us tranquility and peace,
the One who gave us the *rizq* and the *rahmah*—
the sustenance and the compassionate grace—is Allāh.

He made everything
in the *'ālam*, the physical world,
and *'ālamul-arwāh*, the world of pure souls,
into *insān*, into man.
He placed everything, everything
in the *'ālam* and *'ālamul-arwāh* into *insān*—
the *'arsh*, the *kursī*, the *qalam*,

the throne of God, the eye of wisdom,
the pen that writes our destiny,
heaven, and *al-lauhul-mahfūz*,
the tablet upon which man's *nasīb*, his fate, is written.

The One who is the Rabb
gave *insān* everything in perfection,
long life as well as *maut*, death.
Allāh is the One who made us perfectly.
He gave us all the wealth,
all the wealth, the *rahmah* that is the *mubārakāt*,
the grace of the blessing of God's love in all three worlds.
He gave *insān* the exaltedness, splendor, and wisdom
to do *tasbīh*, to glorify, Allāhu ta'ālā Nāyan
with certitude, reverence, and *īmān*.
The One who gave this to us is Allāh.

He is the One who gave us a life without death,
as well as a life with death.
He is the One who gave us a perfect heaven,
as well as an imperfect body and an imperfect hell.
He is the One who gave us *'ilm*, knowledge,
our wisdom, and *īmān* to light the darkness,
as well as the darkness of ignorance and desire.
He is the One who gave us inexhaustible wealth,
giving us the Rahmatul-'ālamīn,
the Mercy of all the universes,
the ultimate, perfect wealth.

He gave us
īmān, certitude, *sabūr*, *shukūr*, *tawakkul*, and *al-hamdu lillāh*,
inner patience, gratitude, trust in God, and
the praise that belongs only to God.
He is the One who gave us the *rahmah*
of the wealth which creates *shukūr*,
and He made it perfect.

O Allāh! You gave us the imperfect *dunyā*, the imperfect world,
the darkness of the world,
its hypnotic delusion,
along with ignorant desires and attachments
that gave us the aspirations
arising from the connection to the *nafs ammārah*—
the seven desires that incite us to do evil—in the *dunyā*.
You gave us the darkness of the bondage of kinship.
You also gave us the perfection of the Light of love and grace.

O the One who is the Giver, Allāhu, *yā* Rabbal-'ālamīn!
We let go of Your perfections
and joyously focused on the imperfections.
We followed the path of destruction,
acting like mind and desire,
letting go of perfection, and reaching out to *maut*, death.
We followed our *nafs*
as they wandered throughout the *dunyā*,
connected to the bondage of kinship,
maya, darkness, hypnotic delusion, lust, anger, and hatred.

Protect us
who follow the path of sin.
Destroy arrogance, karma, and maya.
Make our path straight and make us peaceful.
Destroy the fecal arrogance,
destroy the fanaticism,
destroy the differences, and
grant us the state of tranquility
on peaceful paths.

You have decreed faith, the way to worship You,
sadaqah, charity, fasting, and the hajj pilgrimage.
You have decreed this fast
for wisdom, for perception, for faith, for awareness,

and for the act of perceiving the self
in a way that trusts others as one trusts oneself,
in a way that is appropriate for wisdom and intelligence,
appropriate for perception, awareness, and intelligence,
so the fast can be understood.

God revealed the perfection and the reverence
of this *īmān* to the Rasūl ☻, saying:

Yā Muhammad,
make your *ummah*, your people, understand this.
Tell them to do this *fard*, this obligatory duty.
For those who have declared the Kalimah,[1]
and for those who have *īmān*,
this will be *fard*.
For those who realize this and for those who know Me,
it will be *rahmah*.
If man understands and does this,
if he understands and does duty to all lives,
I will give him My wealth,
I will give him grace.
I will give him the perfection of *īmān* that is the
the Rahmatul-ʿālamīn.

If man allows others to live as he himself does,
with unity, tolerance, and peace,
this will be the greatest of all fasts.
It will be *rahmah*.
It will be what he earns from the *ʿarsh*,
the throne of God.

It will be what he earns from the *ākhirah*,

---

1. Kalimah   The affirmation of faith, *lā ilāha illAllāh*. There is nothing other than You, O God. Only You are God.

the kingdom of God,
the wealth that is beloved to *firdaus*, paradise.
Understand this, *yā* Muhammad,
and tell your *ummah* to do this.
Make them take the straight path on the path of *'ilm*.
Tell them to go on the straight path.
Tell them to study the *'ilm* that is My *rahmah*
and be clear.
This will make it possible for them
to understand the mysterious *'ilm*,
to live in silence, and to have *sabūr* towards everyone.
When man understands that this *'ilm* is his path,
he will know himself and Us.

Make them understand
the Wisdom of Wisdom within wisdom.
Make them understand *Īmān* within *īmān*.
Make them understand the Five Daily Prayers
within the five daily prayers,
and make them pray.
Make them know what is the actual *Sadaqah*
of *Sadaqah* within *sadaqah*,
and make them do it.
Make them perceive what is the actual Fast within the fast,
and make them remain in the state of fasting.
Make them think
of what is the actual Hajj of the Hajj within the hajj,
understand it with *'ilm*, and do it with understanding.
Make them know who it is that is *Insān* within *insān*.
Make them perceive who it is that is the *Kāmil*, the perfection,
within *Insān Kāmil*, the perfected human being.

Make them understand and know the Qutb
that exists as the Light within the *Kāmil*, and *Insān Kāmil*.
Make them perceive the Qutb within the Qutb

and perceive who the Qutb is.
Make them know.
Make them understand who it is
that resplends as the Nūr within the Nūr.
Make them perceive who it is
that resplends as the Ultimate Perfection.
Make them understand what the Treasure is
that exists as Allāh within the Nūr.

He who understands the *rahmah* that abides
within Allāh in whom everything is contained—
anyone who understands—will become
a *mu'min*, a believer,
Insān Kāmil, Dīnul-Islām, the path of purity.
He will never see hell.
He will never see death—
he will never see death or hell.
He will be the one who is eternally alive, *hayāh*,
the one who has received the *rahmah*.
He will be the Life to all lives.
He will live with compassion.

Within that *rahmah*,
he will live with the name 'Abdullāh,
as an *'abd*, a slave, to the Rabb.
He will be the one who does the duty.
Once he realizes the reverent path of *īmān*,
he will live only as an *'abd*, nothing else.
He will be the *'abd* of the Rabb.
Make them perceive this state.

When man perceives this and sees this within,
I will be the *Rahmah*.
When he becomes *Insān* within *insān*,
when he perceives the *insān*

and becomes the *insān*,
I will be the *Insān* within that.
I will be the *Kāmil* within *Insān Kāmil*,
I Myself will be the *'Ilm* within the *'ilm*.
I will exist within it as *Īmān* within *īmān*.

We will be the *Sadaqah* within the *sadaqah*.
I alone will be the *Sadaqah* within the *Sadaqah*
within the *sadaqah*.
I will be the One who is the Fast within the fast.
I will be the One who is the Hajj within the hajj.
I will be the One who exists as the Kalimah within the Kalimah.

We will be the Five Daily Prayers within the five daily prayers.
I will be the One who is seen as Faith within faith.
I will also be the One who is the Eye within the eye.
I will be the One who is the Wealth within the wealth.
I will be the One who is the Nūr within the Nūr.
I will be the One who is the *Qalb* within the *qalb*,
the innermost Heart within the innermost heart.
I will be the Resplendent One within *'ilm*.

I will be the One who is the Qutb within the Qutb.
I will be the One who is Allāh within the Nūr.
Existing as Allāh within Allāh,
I will be the One who received the name Rahmatul-'ālamīn,
the One who does the duty.

Yā Muhammad, recite this to your *ummah*,
to those who have wisdom, to those who have *īmān*,
to those who have certitude,
to those who have become *'ibād*, slaves.
Give this explanation to your *ummah*.

Even if there are some who do not understand this,
tell them to do the five *furūd*,
the five obligatory duties,
so they can perceive this.
Teach them wisdom,
and make them understand through wisdom.

In the *ahādīth*, the traditions of the Prophet ☻,
this is what
Allāhu ta'ālā Nāyan, opening[2] His divine mouth,
explained through grace to the Rasūl, the Messenger ☻,
as the inner meaning of the Qur'ān.
These are the words and the *'ilm* that
Allāhu ta'ālā Nāyan, opening His divine mouth,
explained through grace to the Rasūl ☻
about the fast.

Yā Muhammad,
when I sent down the first *sūrah*, the first verse of the Qur'ān,
to you on Mount Hirā',
I sent this Light and *rahmah*.
When I sent down to you that which is known
as Lailatul-Qadr,
the ray of Light that descended in that Day
was the first Light of the Qur'ān,
the first Light that was imprinted in your *qalb*.
I sent down the Light of Lailatul-Qadr
and opened your *qalb*.

---

2. opening   The Tamil word Bawangal ☻ used here is *malartal*, which literally describes the opening of a flower blossom. Thus, God was opening His divine mouth as softly and sweetly as a flower opens, without any harshness at all.

I transformed the *qalb* of the Ummī[3]
into the *qalb* of *'ilm*, into *rahmah*.
I made it make you remember.
I made it Light.
I did this and revealed it to you so you could understand.
I showed you the *Rahmah* known as Allāhu,
the Light known as Lailatul-Qadr.
I poured that Light into your *qalb*.

Yā Muhammad,
if he who climbs to the top
of the black, granite mountain of the *qalb*
that contains the cave
opens the *bismin-kai*[4] and enters it,
climbs past it to stand within it,
doing *'ibādah* to Me,
I will send down into that *qalb*
the *'ilm* known as Lailatul-Qadr.
I will send down the *'ilm*, the Lailatul-Qadr I sent to you,
to he who does *'ibādah*, *yā* Muhammad.
This ray of Light will resplend
and reverberate in his *qalb*.
Just as I told Angel Gabriel to hold you
and crush you three times,
I will crush in him the three desires: land, woman, and gold,
along with arrogance, karma, maya, desire, anger, sin, and hell.
I will crush the black rocks that originate from bile.

After I crushed those rocks,
I sent you the ray of Light.

---

3. Ummī   The Unlettered One, the Mute One, refers to the Messenger of God ☻, who never read anything except the words of Allāh, and who never said anything except the words of Allāh.
4. *bismin-kai*   the node of flesh on the physical heart where our good and evil deeds are recorded for all time, much like the black box on aircraft

After I sent down the Light,
I made it imprint itself permanently in your *qalb*.
That was the first time I sent down the Lailatul-Qadr
to you as the Day of Light, as the Qur'ān.
Every statement, every word
I sent down into your *qalb* after that, was a ray of Light.
Every ray of Light on Lailatul-Qadr
comes from the Light of Nūr Muhammad.

If you take in everything We send you,
make it your own, and
imprint it in your *qalb*,
when it is revealed from there to the people,
it becomes the Divine Qur'ān,
the Tiru Maray, the Divine Mystical Teaching.
When you reveal it from there,
it becomes the Divine Qur'ān,
the Tiru Maray, the Divine Mystical Teaching.

When it is revealed from the Qur'ān,
each Light exists as a ray.
The ray exists as the *rūh*, the soul.
The *rūh* exists as Light.
That Light exists as *rahmah*.
That *rahmah* exists as perfection.
That perfection exists as the Light of *īmān*, as resplendence.
That resplendence exists as the *dīn*, the path of purity.
That *dīn* is the life to *hayāh*.
That *hayāh* is a mystery.

Existing as the Mystery within the mystery, it is
I alone who come to bestow the *rahmah*
of *Bismillāhir-Rahmānir-Rahīm*
upon all lives.
Yā Muhammad,

explain the meaning of *īmān* to your *ummah*,
open their *'ilm* and their *qalbs*,
break the dark rocks, the black rocks
of the bondage to kinship,
earth, fire, arrogance, karma, maya,
malice, miserliness, selfishness, pride, and jealousy.

The *sūrah*, the form, of *mīm* comes into being
in anyone who breaks apart these dark rocks and
crushes them with his wisdom,
in anyone who breaks apart these rocks
with the Light of *Lām* in *Alif, Lām, Mīm*.[5]
Yā Muhammad,
he becomes Muhammad.

When this form of Muhammad
comes into being,
when he receives this state,
his *'ibādah*, the service and prayer
he performs with an open heart,
will be established.
When the *'ibādah* of
the five daily prayers is established,
the first *sūrah*, the first chapter,
that was given on Lailatul-Qadr
will dawn in his *qalb*.

After that *sūrah* dawns there,
he becomes a *mu'min*, a believer.
After the heart that is Muhammad opens,
he becomes Īmān-Islām.
After the darkness is dispelled,

---

5. *alif, lām, mīm* Arabic letters corresponding to the English letters *a, l, m*. These letters have mystical meanings and powers.

the Light known as Ahamad will dawn.

When you take in everything contained within that Light,
taking in each word We give you
and absorbing it,
after it emerges, it will become My *wilāyāt*,
the *asmā'ul-husnā* of the Qur'ān,
existing as the ninety-nine *wilāyāt*.

The deeds, demeanor, good conduct, virtue,
patience, *sabūr*, *shukūr*, *tawakkul*, *al-hamdu*,
the reverent submission known as *īmān*,
the certitude, and the perfection
will turn into Light within him.
He who acts with My actions is My slave who will live as
a *mu'min*, as Muhammad, as Light, as Nūr, as *rahmah*.
If he puts this into action,
he will be the wealth known as My patience.

O Muhammad, tell them this.
To all who have declared their *īmān* to you,
to all who came here in order to understand Me,
I am revealing the meaning in the outer *furūd*
of all that has been decreed to you.

When this state of
everything I sent down to you
as the Light of Lailatul-Qadr
reaches your *ummah*,
My words, the *ahādīth*, and
the letters of the Qur'ān
will each become a *rūh*, a soul, a ray of Light.
Their *hayāh* will be complete and become *rahmah*.

He who perceives this will become a *mu'min* with *īmān*,
Insān Kāmil, Qutb, Nūr, Nūr Muhammad,
the one who has received the *rahmah* of Allāhu.
He will live as His *'abd.*
Such a man of wisdom will receive My *'ilm* and My *rahmah.*
His *qalb* will exist as Light.
His heart and face will be the heart and face
of the one who has seen Me.
He will do My duty.

Yā Muhammad, say this to your *ummah.*
Tell them this,
show them the clarity of *'ilm,* and make them know it.
Make them reach Us on this path of wisdom.
Make them see Me through
determination, certitude, and patience.
Only then will he obtain the reward.
Only then will he understand this fast.

So said Allāhu ta'ālā Nāyan to the Rasūl ☯,
opening His divine mouth
through grace.

May all of us perceive this.
May we understand the fast, the hajj, *sadaqah,*
faith, the five-times prayer, *īmān,* and worship.
When we understand
the five outer *furūd* and the inner *furūd*
and establish *īmān* after that,
we will become Muhammad ☯.

Then when we leave this cave and emerge from it,
when we leave the cave on Mount Hirā' and emerge
to perform our *'ibādah,*
the Light known as Lailatul-Qadr will descend.

After this resplendent *īmān* and that *sūrah* descend,
after the three desires are destroyed,
the religions will have been destroyed.
When the *'ilm* of the *qalb* becomes Ummī,
everything else will be forgotten
and only Allāh's *'ilm*, His qualities, and His words
will be absorbed there by that *qalb*.
After this is accepted and absorbed,
it will emerge as a word with *hayāh*, a word with life.
Those words will become Light.
We must understand this *'ilm*.

O my brothers and sisters!
O children born with me!
This is the *rahmah* bestowed by Allāhu ta'ālā
upon the Rasūlullāh ☻.
This has been explained in many ways
by the *ahādīth* and in the Qur'ān
as the inner meaning of *'ilm*.
God has explained this.

We have to perceive it and do *tasbīh* to Allāh
according to the inner meaning.
When we understand,
we can know the *rahmah* and the wealth, and
obtain the *rahmah*.
Every child must perceive this and do this,
search for wisdom, and study *'ilm*
according to the inner meaning.
Āmīn. Yā Rabbal-'ālamīn.

O Allāh! May You bestow upon us the grace
of Your blessing and Your *rahmah*.
May You give these children *īmān*
until they are filled to overflowing.

May You open the *qalb* of every child and keep it open.
May You dispel the darkness from their *qalbs*.
After breaking through the black rocks of darkness and delusion,
may You send down the Light of Lailatul-Qadr into their *qalbs*.

Yā Allāh!
May You give them the intention and grant them the grace
to worship and perform *'ibādah* on Your path.
Āmīn. Yā Rabbal-'ālamīn. Āmīn.

Bismillāhir-Rahmānir-Rahīm.
Al-hamdu lillāhi Rabbil-'ālamīn.
Ar-Rahmānir-Rahīm.
Māliki yawmid-dīn.
Iyyāka nā'budu wa iyyāka nasta'īn.
Ihdinas-sirātal-mustaqīm,
sirātal-ladhīna an'amta 'alaihim,
ghairil-maghdūbi 'alaihim wa lad-dāllin,
In the name of Allāh,
the Most Compassionate, the Most Merciful. Praise be to God,
the Cherisher and Sustainer of the worlds.
The Most Compassionate, the Most Merciful.
Master of the Day of Judgment.
Thee alone do we worship and only Thine aid do we seek.
Show us the straight way,
the way of those on whom Thou hast bestowed Thy grace,
those whose (portion) is not wrath, and who go not astray.
Āmīn.

As-salāmu 'alaikum wa rahmatullāhi wa barakātuhu kulluhu.
May all the peace and mercy and blessings of God be upon you.
Go and complete your fast.
As-salāmu 'alaikum wa rahmatullāhi wa barakātuhu kulluhu.
May all the peace and mercy and blessings of God be upon you.

A'ūdhu billāhi minash-shaitānir-rajīm.
I seek refuge in God from the accursed satan.
Bismillāhir-Rahmānir-Rahīm.
In the name of God, the Most Compassionate, the Most Merciful.

THE DAY OF MEETING ALLĀH
July 29, 1981

Bismillāhir-Rahmānir-Rahīm. In the name of Allāh, the Most Compassionate, the Most Merciful. *As-salāmu 'alaikum wa rahmatullāhi wa barakātuhu.* May the peace and compassionate grace and blessings of God be upon you.

May all praise and glory be to Allāh! Allāhu ta'ālā Nāyan is the One who is the Giver of Immeasurable Grace, the One who is Incomparable Love. May His mercy be ever merciful! May we understand His *ni'mah* as a *ni'mah*, understanding His beneficial blessing as a boon. May His *qudrah*, His power, His mercy, His *rahmah*, His compassionate grace, His *wilāyāt*, His actions and duties, be revealed in His qualities! May His actions and qualities, His *wilāyāt*, His *rahmah*, and His compassion be within Him in purity and mercy! May the *rahmah* of the speech, words, actions, and duty of the One who is the Giver of Immeasurable Grace, the One who is Incomparable Love, be within Him as purity!

The One who is the Giver of Immeasurable Grace, the One who is Incomparable Love, the rare, great Light that is Allāhu, instituted His laws, commandments, and the *'ilm*, the divine knowledge, of the *rahmah* through the 124,000 *ambiyā'*, prophets, and the *aqtāb*. The *'ilm* belonging to His compassionate grace was sent down through them. The Rahmatul-'ālamīn, the Mercy for all the universes, was sent down to make the *qalbs* of *insān*, the innermost hearts of humankind, absolutely pure and to transform them into the *rahmah*. To make the *qalbs* of all the children of Adam ⊚ pure, God taught His commandments through His prophets, sending down worship, *'ibādah*, the five daily prayers, the *salawāt*, the *salām*, *dhikr*, and *fikr* in order to open our *qalbs* and make them pure.

He sent down the *bahrul-'ilm*, the sea of divine knowledge, and the blessing of the Rahmatul-'ālamīn. Today, this is what we are praying to receive.

The ultimate clarification of our request is that the Qur'ān Sharīf tells us today is Lailatul-Qadr, a day we can meet God.

It has been said that the twenty-seventh day of the month of Ramadān, the month of fasting, is the day that the ray of Light was sent down to the Rasūl☻, that today is the day of the ray of Light. The proof is in the Qur'ān Sharīf. This was sent down to the Rasūl☻ by Allāh's command, by His decree. He showed him the Light.

For those of the children of Adam☻ who are the *mu'minūn*, the believers, for those who have gained perfect and pure *īmān* and certitude, this is a time of *salāmah*, of safety and security, when their *qalbs* are filled to the brim with these treasures, when they gain the *salāmah* of exalted qualities during their lives, when they receive the purity from Allāh in the *ākhiratuz-zamān*, the time of the kingdom of God, when they achieve the victory—the *rahmah* and the wealth of the victory. This is the day they meet Allāh, commune with Him, and speak to Him. The day known as Lailatul-Qadr has been exalted and sent down to the Rasūl☻ as proof.

When we focus on what Lailatul-Qadr is in the month of Ramadān, we have to think of how Allāhu ta'ālā Nāyan's *sabab*[1]— the fast of Ramadān, the prayers of Ramadān, the *salām* and the *salawāt* of Ramadān, the *'ibādah* of Ramadān, and the silent *dhikrs* of Ramadān—has to be. We have to think of this.

Think of the state in which a child lives and does *tasbīh* to Allāh when it is first conceived in its mother's womb and growing into a fetus. Think of the state in which it fasts. Think of the state in which it breathes. Think of the state in which it lives with the

---

1. Allāhu ta'ālā Nāyan's *sabab*   the means of reaching Him

malā'ikah, the angels. Think of how it lives for nine or ten months doing *tasbīh*. Think of the state in which it exists for nine or ten months.

That is why this day of the fast can also be called the Day of *Taubah*, the Day of Repentance. The fast is to be still and to do *tasbīh*.

The person who fasts should fast and perform these prayers and *dhikrs* just as the fetus abides in silence doing *tasbīh*, and grows without taking a breath, without hearing outer sound, without outer eyesight, without outer incentive, without outer speech, without outer words. Does it possess a mattress? Does it possess a bed? Does it possess a *musallā*, a prayer mat? No! The fetus performs *tasbīh* curled up where it is.

A man must fast and perform *tasbīh* in a similar state during Ramadān without outer sound, without outer speech, without outer distraction, without outer intention, without outer eyesight. He must live as a child lives in the womb. He must reach his fully developed state just as a child does *tasbīh* in the womb. He must live as he lived before he came out into the world.

The fast of Ramadān must be diligently kept in that way. He who keeps the fast like this will successfully complete the fast and obtain the beauty just as a child obtains beauty, and he will commune with God just as a child communes with God. Through this fast, he too will commune with Allāh and the Rasūl ☺. Allāh's ray of Light will descend upon such a person on Lailatul-Qadr just as it descended upon the Rasūl ☺. He will speak to God through that ray of Light, he will speak to Him from a state of silence.

It is then that he will live in the *dunyā* having become a child to the angels, to the prophets, to the *aqtāb*, to Allāh, to the *rusul*, the messengers, to the people of wisdom, to all who have *īmān*. He will have become a baby. The heavenly beings will cradle that baby in their arms. The angels will cradle him, the *aqtāb* will cradle him, the *auliyā'* and the *ambiyā'* will cradle him and kiss him.

They will hold him and embrace him with the Light. That day will be the day Allāh will hold him and embrace him. That day will be the day this Light will hold him and embrace him. That will be the day he is embraced by purity. The day in which he is embraced like that is called Lailatul-Qadr. That is the day in which the ray of Light will come down to him. That will be the day he meets Allāh.

He will have become a newborn. He will not see the world, maya, karma, sin, anger, *self-business*, differences, or separation. All that emanates from Allāh will emanate from that child. He will look at everyone with peace and equality. He will be a child that plays with everyone. Snakes will not harm him. Tigers will not kill him. Poisonous creatures will not bite him.

He will abide with the Reality in which the world does not exist, with the Reality that has no connection to maya, with the Reality that sin cannot touch, with the Reality that has no envy, with the Reality that has no deceit or treachery, with the Reality that has no anger, with the Reality that contains none of the things that desire land, gold, or woman, with the Reality that has no blood ties, with the Reality that has no cow, no calf, no house, no possessions, no property.

No karma or sin will touch him. None of the hells will touch him. Neither birth nor death will touch him. It is said that his fast is a fully developed state in which nothing can touch him.

If the fast is kept in this way, if he keeps at least one such fast in his lifetime, he will intermingle with the Light of Lailatul-Qadr on this day.

Precious children, jeweled lights of my eyes, *insān* has been formed of twenty-eight *hurūf*, or letters. Of these twenty-eight letters, one is the day of his birth, one is the day of his death. The day of birth and the day of death are actually only one day— that day is the day of delusion, the day of darkness. That is the *ammāvāsay*, the dark of the moon, Adam's day, the day Adam ☻ and Eve ☻ were deluded.

The day the Light appeared, the day the rays of Light began to expand, are the twenty-seven other letters. Allāhu ta'ālā Nāyan formed *insān* with those twenty-seven letters. Those twenty-seven letters are the twenty-seven constellations that exist in his body.

Each letter is a constellation that is clearly evident in his body.

He who understands the influences and the effects of the constellations will understand the constellation connected to earth, the constellation connected to *maut*, death, the constellation connected to gold and property, the constellation belonging to the *nafs*, the constellation belonging to the *malā'ikah*, the constellation belonging to the jinns, the constellation belonging to the fairies, the constellation belonging to the *auliyā'*, the constellation belonging to the *ambiyā'*, the constellation belonging to the *aqtāb*, the constellation belonging to *'ilm*, the constellation belonging to al-Quddūs, the Holy One—the luminous constellations belonging to Allāh, in the fully-developed heavenly state.

These are the constellations that are clearly evident in the eighteen thousand universes. All the constellations exist within *insān*. When man was being created, he was created with these constellations, these letters. With these constellations, with these twenty-seven letters, Allāhu ta'ālā Nāyan opened and revealed the 6,666 *āyāt*, the 6,666 verses, of the Qur'ān.

How many sections there are in one constellation! They are countless. This is what He has revealed.

The day of the twenty-seventh letter, the day of reaching Allāh, is the day known as Lailatul-Qadr. The day the Light of Nūr Muhammad⊕ descends, the day the Light is seen, the day the completion is attained, the day of merging, is called Lailatul-Qadr. It is said that this is the day the purity coming from Allāh is seen.

When this perfect Lailatul-Qadr is completed—the fast, the *'ibādah*, the *dhikr*—he will abide in his *qalb* just as a child abides in the womb. If he keeps the fast in the room that is his *qalb*, that will be his shrine. His mother's belly was once his house of worship. Now his *qalb* will be the shrine, the room in which he prays and worships. His fast, prayer, meditation, five daily prayers, *'ibādah*, *salawāt*, *salām*, his *dhikr*, and *fikr*, and his praise of Allāh will originate from there. He will worship God in the house of his *qalb*. He will fast there. He will pray there. He will worship there. He will do *tasbīh* there. It is there that the *salawāt* will reverberate. It is there that he will say his *salām*. When he performs those actions from there, that is the day he will see the ray of Light come down.

The Light of Nūr Muhammad ☻ will come down. It will come down from his *'arsh* into his *kursī*, from the throne of God on the crown of his head into the eye of wisdom in the center of his forehead. It will emerge from the *kursī*—the Qutbiyyah[2] will emerge from the *kursī*. The *'ilm* and the Light known as the Qutb ☻ will emerge from the Qutbiyyah. That is the eye that sees the *'ālam* and *'ālamul-arwāh*, this world and the world of pure souls.

That will be the day the *'ālam*, *'ālamul-arwāh*, and everything in the eighteen thousand universes will be illumined. That will be the day he knows himself, the day he praises Allāh, the day he needs to reach the *rahmah*. That is the day he attains purity.

That day is the twenty-seventh day of the twenty-eight letters, the day of the Light known as Nūr Muhammad ☻.

When Allāhu ta'ālā Nāyan created Adam ☻, he fused the Light of Nūr Muhammad ☻ into his forehead. That is the day the Light was opened. When the Light opened, God explained everything to Adam ☻. Everything became clear and luminous. That was Lailatul-Qadr, the day of all days when everything was made known. It was that Light.

That is the kind of worship and fast we must perform, the house of worship we must understand. A child does *tasbīh* from within the belly of its mother. That is the house in which it lives. On the fast days, we must remain in the *qalb*—the shrine must be our house, the *qalb* must be a house of worship in which we do *tasbīh* and complete the fast. That is the twenty-seventh day.

He who successfully completes it will experience the purity known as Lailatul-Qadr. That will be the day the Light comes down. He will see the *rahmah* that will come down into his *'ilm* while he is still alive.

You must think of this.

Today is the Lailatul-Qadr the Qur'ān Sharīf has described.

---

2. Qutbiyyah   the state of the Qutb ☻, *Pahut Arivu*, the sixth level of wisdom, the state that explains the truth of God to the human soul

This is the time and this is the way. Today we understand this in many ways, according to our own current state. The state that exists today, the state that exists in these hundred years contains meanings that we have come to understand over many hundreds of years. There are many ways.

However, we must understand *'ilm* from within *'ilm*. We must understand wisdom from within wisdom. We must understand truth from within truth. We must understand *īmān* from within *īmān*. We must understand worship from within worship. We must understand the five daily prayers from within the five daily prayers. We must understand *dhikr* from within *dhikr*. We must understand the *salām* from within the *salām*. We must understand the *salawāt* from within the *salawāt*. We must understand the Qutb ☺ from within the Qutb ☺. We must understand man from within man. We must understand the Nūr from within the Nūr. We must understand Allāh from within Allāh. That Light will be understood only from within that Light.

That is the day *Insān Kāmil* becomes a *mu'min*, the day the perfected human being becomes a believer. When he understands *'ilm*, he becomes a *mu'min*. He will understand his birth and his death. On that day, he will understand whether he will get the *ākhirah*, the kingdom of God, or *dunyā*, the world; whether he will get *jahannam*, the lowest hell, or heaven. Then he will understand. On Judgment Day, he will know which group is his.

He will know the answers to the questions in the *qabr*, the grave, whether he died as a *mu'min*, a believer, or whether he died as a *kāfir*, someone who obscures the truth. Will the investigation of his good and evil deeds in the *qabr* discover good, or evil? Will his house in the *ākhirah* be a house of goodness, or a house of evil? Will Allāh's judgment end in goodness for him, or evil? Will he get heaven or hell on the Day of Qiyāmah, the Day of Resurrection? Is he an *insān*, or a *hayawān*, a human being, or a beast? He will understand the meanings of these questions. That will be the Day in which he will understand.

It is through this *daulat*, this wealth, that he will understand

and reach a state of death before he dies, a state of judgment before he is judged, a day of questioning before the Day of Questioning. He will understand and die as a *mu'min*. He will join the group of the *mu'minūn*, those who have *īmān*. He will live as one of the *ummah* from the lineage of Muhammad ☻. He will live as an *'abd* who has the love of Allāh. He will grow and his *hayāh*, his life, will be that of one who does *tasbīh* to Allāh. He will surrender to Him.

We must understand this. In His explanation in the Qur'ān Sharīf, Allāhu ta'ālā Nāyan has shown us a very complex way to understand this, as well as an easy way, along with ordinary ways. Allāh has shown us that as we dig deeper and deeper, going further and further, there will be revealed more clear and detailed ways. We must realize these states. He has shown us.

We must realize these states. We see the Qur'ān according to the state in which we live. If we are to understand the Qur'ān, we need *tauhīd*.[3] If we do not have *tauhīd* when we endeavor to understand the Qur'ān, we will not understand its greatness. Understanding the Arabic language is easy. *Tauhīd* is mandatory. Without it, we will not understand the Qur'ān's greatness. Therefore, when we recite the Qur'ān, we must endeavor to know its greatness and meaning. Through doing so, we can know the greatness of Allāh, and the greatness of the Rasūl ☻, the greatness of *'ilm*, their depth, their vastness, their expanse, and their magnitude.

When we recite the Qur'ān without understanding, it becomes merely something to study, an analysis of history. It is like reading a *storybook*. It is like reading religious stories from a religious point of view, like reading a story in another language. It is like reading a story minus the feeling of awe. It is like a state of celebrating joy and sorrow while laughing and playing—without fear or awe.

We must recite the Qur'ān with absolute certitude. Allāh has given it as a thing of greatness. We must keep that thing of greatness in a great place. We must regard it with great respect. We must go deep into it, digging ever deeper and deeper.

---

3. *tauhīd*   the affirmation of the unity of Allāh; the state of oneness without any trace of duality; the indivisible and absolute Oneness of God

My love you my children, my sons and daughters. In order to know the greatness of the One who possesses neither bias nor prejudice, we must stand in a place without bias or prejudice, and then look. God is the One who stands beyond what is beyond the scriptures and doctrines. We must go beyond them, stand with Him, and see as He sees. He is the One without envy, jealousy, or treachery. We have to stand without those evils, transcend them, and see what lies beyond.

Allāhu is the All-Powerful, Perfect Being, the Resonance that transcends religious scriptures. He is absolute Purity; the One who pervades and dwells within all lives; the One who has created all life; the One who feeds each and every living being; the One who summons every life; the One who questions every life; the One who gives every life a place in which to live; the One who summons each life, awakens it, and asks the questions later, at the end. He gives what needs to be given in an exact and perfect way. He is the Embracer. We need to know the qualities of such a Nāyan, such an Allāh, with such greatness. He who goes to that place is a *mu'min*.

Until that time, he will be the reader of a *storybook*. We who are in the *bahrul-'ilm* must think. We must think of Lailatul-Qadr, Īmān-Islām, and the five and the six obligatory duties.

When Allāhu ta'ālā Nāyan was creating man with the twenty-eight letters, He placed the eighteen thousand universes within that creation. When He took hold of the handful of earth, within it were the essence, the energy, and the qualities of earth. When He took hold of the air, there were many tens of millions of colors and hues within it. He placed the energies and qualities of water within man. It was the same with air, the same with earth, the same with fire, the same with ether.

God created man, placing within him the five elements, the *malā'ikah*, Gabriel☉, Michael☉, Raphael☉, Israel☉, Rūqā'il☉, the two angels on his shoulders, the heavenly messengers, the heavenly angels, the Light of the Rasūl☉, Nūr Muhammad☉, hell and heaven, everything. *Sharr* and *khair*; *sirr* and *sifāt*; *halāl* and *harām*—evil and goodness; the mystery and its outer form; the permissible and the forbidden; fragrant smells and foul smells, fragrant things and foul-smelling things; bright things and dark things; wise things and ignorant things; clear things and unclear things; the *hayawān*, the animals, the monkeys, the dogs, the cats; the viruses, the cells, the energies; *shaitān* and *shaitān's* qualities; grace and the qualities of grace; lust, anger, malice, sin; goodness, exalted qualities, the actions, conduct, and demeanor of Allāh, Allāh's compassion and patience—everything was mixed together and combined in the *sūrah* of *insān*, in the body of man.

The meaning of this is that God created everything—He created everything—and then placed all of it within man.

Allāh has said:

> I have created everything and placed it within man. In man, *sharr* and *khair* are in the *tawakkul*, the responsibility, of Allāh. I have created both evil and goodness in a state of *tawakkul*. Both must be understood and known. Man must discard one of the two while accepting the other and acting with it. I have also created within him the wisdom, the ability, and the *'ilm* with which he can do that. I have created My ninety-nine *wilāyāt* and the three thousand gracious qualities for him. I have given them to him.
>
> I have placed My kingdom and the qualities of My kingdom within him. I have given him all of My wealth. All of his wealth exists within Me.
>
> I am a secret to him. He is a secret to Me. If he is the one who knows Me, he will give a clear explanation of Me. Since I am the One who knows him, I will give a clear explanation of him. He has been conceived within Me, become an embryo within Me, and emerged from Me. I created him from within Myself. He knew Me and took form

within Me as an embryo. I revealed him from within Myself. He was born within Me.

On the day that he conceives Me as an embryo within himself, he will understand Me. On the day he makes Me an embryo and gives birth to Me from within himself, his Qiyāmah, his hell, and his sins will be abolished. They will all be abolished.

He will become the leader of My kingdom. He will become the *bādushāh* of My wealth. I will exist as the Light of his wisdom, doing everything and giving him everything he needs. As the Light of his wisdom, I will be the One doing everything for him and revealing everything to him.

I will exist as the inexhaustibly abundant Treasure that does everything for him and reveals everything to him. I will be the One doing *khidmah*, or service, for him. If he conceives Me as an embryo within himself, I will be the One doing *khidmah* for him. And because he has become an embryo within Me, he will now do *khidmah* for Me.

He must do My duty. Why? I raised him and now he must serve Me. If he has conceived Me as an embryo within himself, I must serve him. That is *khair*, good. That will be his *khair*.

If that which is *sharr*, or evil, within him, has not been understood and discarded from within him, that is what becomes karma, what is connected to him. If he places his *tawakkul* in Me, discards evil, and accepts the good, he will reap the reward.

That is what Allāh has said, in a profoundly deep way. His explanations are profoundly deep, and we must understand them with profoundly deep *'ilm*. He is very gradually training us. There are twenty-seven letters that we must understand in twenty-seven ways.

Twenty-seven. Beginning at the time we are in the womb, there are twenty-seven ways that we must pray. They are steps. There is so much that we must understand in every constellation, every letter. Allāhu taʿālā Nāyan sent down our Rasūl ☮ as a *mu'min*, so we could understand. Twenty-five prophets are described in the Qur'ān Sharīf. Beyond that, there are the *ahādīth*, and our common knowledge of the 124,000 prophets. They are His representatives. Whom did He reveal? His representatives. They are called His representatives.

We have been instructed to believe absolutely without doubt in Allāh, Allāh's *ambiyā'*, the *rusul*, and the *aqtāb*. The *aqtāb* are a treasure that Allāh revealed. They reveal Allāh, the Rasūl ☮, His Light, His speech, and His *daulat*. Allāh has told us about His saints, His prophets, and His representatives. Those who clearly reveal things about Allāh to us are called His representatives. To know this without doubt and to accept Him—this is the meaning. They have told us what kind of Being is Allāh; what kind of Being is the Rahmān, the Most Compassionate; what kind of Being is the Rahīm, the Most Merciful; what kind of Being is the Karīm, the Most Generous.

Anyone who clearly reveals Him, His *daulat*, His qualities, His actions, His *wilāyāt*, and His *rahmah* is called His representative. That is the reason the 124,000 prophets were sent down. Although only twenty-five of them are described in the Qur'ān Sharīf, 124,000 prophets have been mentioned in the *ahādīth* and many other places.

We who are human beings, each one of us, must think of this. Those who possess the seal and the greatness that is His *rahmah*, those who can reveal Allāh and the Rasūl ☮, the fathomless meanings of their words, their expansive wisdom, the duty they did throughout the land and their exalted compassionate qualities are rare treasures.

"Those treasures brought peace and tranquility to all lives," explained Allāh. God has opened His divine mouth through grace and said, "All who help the treasures are My representatives." This has been said to the Rasūl ☽.

We who are believers, human beings, and children of Adam ☽ must realize this. We must realize this and endeavor to open the explanation within us.

For example, although there may be a thousand of us or even ten thousand of us, we would look for a doctor, would we not, for a pain in our stomach, a pain in our heart, a pain in our womb, a pain in our eye, a pain in our nose, a pain in our ear, a pain in our mouth, a pain in our chest. There are doctors to treat each body part in those who are ill, are there not? We visit that doctor and take care of the matter. Did we know what was happening? If we did, we ourselves could have treated the illness. No, we did not know, did we?

It is like this that we must understand the Qur'ān Sharīf. We must know it and we must study it. Knowing oneself is also like that. To understand oneself, to study and understand what is within oneself is like looking for a doctor to cure our illnesses. We must search for the *'ilm* known as the Rahmatul-'ālamīn and study it. If we study this *daulat*, we can become a doctor capable of curing countless diseases. It is like this. Allāh's *rahmah* is a great history. It is very deep. A deep subject must be studied deeply. A worthy subject must be studied in a worthy manner.

Yet we think we have studied it by reciting it in another language. If all of us have studied the language, the scripture, and the path, why are we still looking for a doctor? That is a separate subject. It exists as the Path within the path. It is a Path within the Path within the path. It exists as the Explanation within the explanation. It exists as the Purity within the purity. It exists as the *Rahmah* within the *rahmah*. It exists as the Nūr within the Nūr, the Light within the Light. It is the *daulat* that exists as the King of the Wealth of Wisdom within *īmān*. It is Purity within purity.

We must study the *'ilm* that exists as Allāh within Allāh. It is extremely deep. May we think of this. We must study Allāh's *'ilm* for our *hayāh*, our lives, our worship and *'ibādah*, our *dhikr* and *fikr*, our five daily prayers and everything else. If we study this *'ilm*, regarding it as our happiness and freedom, it will be *'ilm* that can bring peace to everyone, it will be *'ilm* that can cure their illnesses, *'ilm* that can feed them wisdom, *'ilm* that can show compassion. That is what we need to study. We must study the *'ilm* that can cure our illnesses. Yet, despite all the *'ilm* we have studied so far, we still have to look for a doctor.

If we are to study that *'ilm*, we need to know who is the One that possesses the *'ilm*. He is the Guardian, our Protector. He is the Guardian capable of protecting us and our wealth. We must study that *'ilm*—Allāh's *'ilm*. It is because He is the Guardian protecting us and our wealth that we must study His *'ilm*, qualities, actions, and state. It is His *'ilm*.

Our wealth is with Him. Our freedom is with Him. Our life is with Him. Our *rahmah* is with Him. The *qudrah* is with Him. The *wilāyāt* are with Him. Therefore, if we are to gain that wealth, we must go to Him to learn it and obtain it. It is only if we learn it and obtain it from Him that we will be among those who have obtained their freedom. We will have material wealth, the wealth of the soul, the wealth of *gnānam*, divine wisdom, the wealth of meaning, the wealth of compassion, the wealth of patience, the wealth of *sabūr*, *shukūr*, *tawakkal*, and *al-hamdu lillāh*, praising Him. Then we will obtain the three thousand kinds of divine wealth known as His Rahmatul-'ālamīn.

We must learn from Him in order to obtain from Him the *'ilm*, the worship, the *'ibādah*, and the five daily prayers that can earn that wealth. We must study this and understand *'ilm*, jeweled lights of my eyes. That is what is *heavy*.

He who accomplishes that becomes the doctor for the soul. He is the doctor who has worked hard for the liberation of his soul. On the day his soul is liberated, he will live in freedom. He will be released from slavery. He has obtained liberation for his soul. This is the teaching, the *'ilm*, the *daulat*, the divine *rahmah*,

Allāh's blessing. We must endeavor to obtain it. We must endeavor to study this *'ilm*. It is difficult. It is heavy and it is difficult.

We must finish studying it amidst many hardships. May we endeavor to do this. Precious jeweled lights of my eyes, this is the teaching.

Before us, Allāhu ta'ālā Nāyan sent down the *ambiyā'* and the *aqtāb* with the four religious books because all the eighteen thousand universes are within us. He sent down four kinds of *ambiyā'*, *auliyā'*, and *aqtāb*. From the time of Adam ☉ until today, and until the Day of Qiyāmah after Qiyāmah, everything He has manifested, everything He has created, has been combined within us. Everything has been combined with the eighteen thousand universes.

We see muscles, skin, blood, a form, two eyes, two ears, a nose, a mouth, two hands, and two legs; or we see four-legged creatures with eyes and noses; or we see the wings on the birds—two-legged creatures with wings, legs, and bodies. No matter how we look at them, their bodies contain earth, fire, water, air, and ether. Those bodies contain earth, water, air, fire, the colors of the sky, and the maya that are combined with them. We can see the body in any state. The only difference is in the skin. If we peel off the skin, we will see bloody flesh. We will see basically the same bones, flesh, tissue, marrow, and skin. These things are there in whatever we look at. They exist in the same manner in a man, in a cow, and in a goat.

We are creatures containing blood. God, Allāhu ta'ālā Nāyan turned water into blood, He turned the blood into a clot, He turned the clot of blood into a bit of flesh, He nourished the bit of flesh in four ways, and lovingly revealed it as a body. We have been formed from water. We grew from a clot of blood, a bit of flesh. Let us think of this.

This is how everything has grown. Yet, it is not about this part [the form]. It is about what is within it. This is the cause, within it is the effect, and within that effect is the *rahmah* of Allāh, the Supreme Being who is the Cause of all things. The One who controls the cause is God, the Creator. Let us think of this.

One is the cause, the other is the effect. The One who exists beyond them is the Supreme Being who is the Cause of all things. God, the Creator controls everything, He is the Being inside everything.

It is to make this understood that Allāh sent down so many *ambiyā'* and *aqtāb*. He brought this into the Qur'ān Sharīf and made it complete. He described the history of what had happened in the past and the history of all that was going to happen in the future.

> *Yā* Muhammad, may you make them all the children of Adam, the lineage of Abraham, the *ummah* of Muhammad. I created creation from the children of Adam. I taught faith and patience through Abraham. O Muhammad, I opened My house through your *ummah*—I opened My house and I placed it in their care. O Muhammad, I will call them unto Myself as your *ummah*.

It was also at this time that God said:

> Tell them to make *taubah*, to repent, for their mistakes. Tell this to your *ummah*. I will be the One who looks at the mistakes of the others. Tell them that each of them must look at his own mistakes. I am the One who hears, sees, and investigates the mistakes of others. Tell your *ummah* to look at their own mistakes and to make *taubah* for them. Tell them to do *taubah* for their own mistakes, their own thoughts, their own words, their own faults. I will be the One who looks into the affairs of the others. I am the One who judges. I will do that. That day is My Day.
>
> This day is his day, man's day, the day that

belongs to your *ummah*. Today is man's day, a good day. That Day will be My Judgment Day. Tell him to do good today. Today is not the Day that will come in the future—that is Judgment Day. Today is a good day for him. Because today is his day, tell him to do *tasbīh* today. Tell him to do *tasbīh* and *taubah*. Tell your *ummah* that they must stop making those mistakes.

All the days that we have thought of as being today, today, today, today, and today, are all *taubah* days, while we are still alive. These are the good days. We should not think, *Tomorrow, tomorrow!* We must think, *Today, today!* The day we do *taubah* is a good day for us. Tell them to do this. Tell each one. They have only today. Tell them not to think of tomorrow. Tomorrow is My Day. Today is his day. Tell him that. Today is his day, tomorrow is My Day, the Day of Judgment. Tell this to your *ummah*. This breath is his breath. Tell him to do *taubah* for it. Tomorrow's breath is My breath. He does not understand what I have for him. Tomorrow could be My Judgment Day. Tell him to correct this breath. This is his time. O Muhammad, tell this to your *ummah*.

God laid open and explained the 6,666 *āyāt* and countless *ahādīth* in this state. We must think of this.

God said to him:

That is why I ultimately told you to say this to your *ummah*. I sent down the Kalimah and a *sunnah*[4] for each *nabī*, each prophet. I sent down

---

4. *sunnah*   the words, deeds, and actions attributed to the messengers of God, peace be upon them

guidelines for health and rules for hygiene so that the people could live healthily without disease. Today, the children of Adam have forgotten health and hygiene. They have lost health and hygiene, and that is why they are sick. Their bodies are sick, their eyes are sick, their eyesight is sick, their voices are sick, their tongues are sick, their noses are sick, their *qalbs* are sick, their arms and legs are sick. They live like sick people.

That is why, *yā* Muhammad, I have told your *ummah* to do the *wudū'*, the ablution, in sixteen steps, so they can live as healthy sixteen-year-olds. How can that Light be generated? Tell them to do *wudū'* in sixteen steps before praying to Me, O Muhammad.

The *wudū'* we perform on the outside is accomplished by taking water and cleansing the hands, mouth, teeth, nose, face, eyes, arms, head, neck, ears, and feet. Washing the hands and the feet is the ordinary *wudū'*.

The *wudū'* for worshipping Allāh requires that we do *wudū'* in the *qalb* in sixteen steps. If we can purify our *qalbs* like that, we will never be sick people. We will not have eye diseases or illnesses that cause delirium.

We will not be people whose noses smell bad—we will not smell offensive, we will be fragrant. We must be transformed into people whose mouths, sweat, urine, and feces do not smell offensive. We must be transformed into people who hear no evil sounds in their ears, who think no evil thoughts, who indulge in no evil pleasures. We must be transformed into people whose sweat and body do not smell offensive. We must be transformed into people free of inner germs, illnesses, and diseases.

Allāh has said:

> Thus, please tell them to perform those sixteen

steps of *wuḍū'*—it will give them the brightness and beauty of youth. Tell them to do this *wuḍū'* at every *waqt*, every moment in time, before they do *tasbīḥ* to Me, before they pray to Me. This is the *wuḍū'* of the *qalb*.

Precious children, jeweled lights of my eyes, this is not what we do when we only wash with water. We must wash ourselves in Allāh's *'ilm*.

It is not only about washing with water, we must wash ourselves in Allāh's words. It is not only about washing our noses and faces with water, we must wash ourselves with the *raḥmah* of Allāh. It is not only about washing with water, it is washing our *qalbs* with faith in Allāh. It is not only about washing with water, we must wash our *qalbs* with Allāh's qualities.

It is not only washing with water, we must be among those who wash themselves with Allāh's actions. It is not only washing with water, we must be among those who wash themselves with Allāh's *sabūr*. It is not only washing with water, we must must be among those who wash themselves and do *tasbīḥ* with *shukūr* amidst the good and the bad in life. All who wash themselves like this will be among those who wash themselves with Allāh's *tawakkul*. We will not wash only with water, we will be those who wash themselves with *al-ḥamdu lillāh*—all praise is Your praise! We will not wash only with water, we will be those who live as slaves and who wash themselves with the Light of Muhammad ☮. We must surrender.

These are the sixteen steps of *wuḍū'*, of cleansing ourselves with the Kalimah. We will wash not only with water, we will be among those who wash themselves with absolute *īmān*, *īmān* that contains no doubt whatsoever.

These are the sixteen steps of *wuḍū'* for the *qalb*. This is done for the *qalb*. We must know this *wuḍū'*. If we perform this *wuḍū'*, we will not experience the diseases of the *dunyā*, the diseases of the *nafs*, the diseases of prejudice and bias, the diseases of *shaiṭān*, the diseases of the demons, the diseases of the *nafs ammārah* and anger, the diseases carried by viruses, cells, and the air, the diseases of the evil thoughts of *shaitān*. We must discard all the diseases like this.

If we understand, we can obtain perfect health. That is perfect health. If we endeavor to perform this *wudū'* before we do *tasbīh* to Allāh, that is worship. That worship belongs to Allāh. We must understand how to cleanse this house of the *qalb* as it is described in the Qur'ān Sharīf. We must do this *wudū'* and this *'ibādah*. This is what Allāh has told us. This is the way we must do it.

The day that we have finished doing what we need to do is called Lailatul-Qadr. We must do *tasbīh*. It must all be understood.

God has said:

> O Muhammad, I have given you five *waqts*, five times of prayer, so this can be understood. I have decreased the *waqts* from fifty to five. May you make your followers realize these five *waqts*.
>
> They have earth disease, fire disease, water disease, and air disease. They have the disease of the desire for earth, woman, and property. They have the blood disease, blood tie disease, mind disease, arrogance disease, and the karma disease. They have the jealousy disease, the envy disease, and the gossip disease. They have the treachery disease, the deceit disease, and the doubt disease. They have the bigotry disease, the "I" disease, and the "you" disease. They have the disease known as desire and the disease known as attachment. All of these diseases have attached themselves to them.
>
> May they understand these diseases, cut them away, and gain perfect health. Man is My wealth and I am his. I have shown him the reason he must live in a healthy way in order to understand My history.

I have shown him the examples of earth, fire, water, air, gold, silver, and woman who is My *rahmah*. I have shown him how the women who are My *rahmah* have become beautiful. Even if a man cannot find peace in Me, he should at least be able to see the example of the women who are My *rahmah*. May he understand them, find clarity in his life, and peace. I have shown him these examples so that he can do this.

This is the reason I created Eve after I created Adam. Because Adam could not fully worship Me when he was alone, I created women from *rahmah* and made them beautiful, so that man could look at them and realize, so he too could know Me, so he too could be comforted. That is why I gave him a mate. I sent down women from My *rahmah*, and showed man the reason for it, by enabling women to serve him. The *khidmah* done by a woman would enable him to understand. May he realize Me by seeing how a woman obtains peace from both joy and sorrow. May he realize by seeing the hardship a woman suffers during pregnancy. May he realize how much hardship comes to a woman from his little moment of pleasure. May he realize how much she serves him in the midst of so much difficulty. May he realize how she does *khidmah* to him.

I have created everything just as I have created him. I am his Servant, am I not? No matter what he does, no matter how much he makes Me suffer, I serve him without hurting him. May he at least realize and know My duty through the example shown by women. That is why I am giving this explanation. I have made woman beautiful to serve him. I have made man beautiful to serve Me.

I have given this example so that he can become aware and realize this. That is the reason I created My *'ilm*.

Man is My property. I have made women beautiful from the *rahmah* as My property. Man's house, his jungle, his body are also My property. His breath and his speech are My property. All the things he experiences are My things. Make him realize this. I have sent into him My *'ilm*, My wisdom, and My qualities so he can realize this. I have buried them within him. I brought the messengers into being to reveal this. Yet he does not realize.

O Muhammad! Make them your *ummah*. This is why I made the fifty *waqts* of prayer into five *waqts*. I have made those five *waqts fard*, obligatory, for you. I made the *furūd* into commandments and gave them to you. At least, make man realize that much.

First make him believe in Me. Make him realize that I am his property. Make him realize that I am his freedom. Make him realize that I am his wealth. He has to know Me if I am to make what I have into his rightful property. I do not take his property and turn it into My property. When he understands Me and asks Me, I give him his property. Only what I dispense belongs to him. He cannot dispense it. My property is Mine—he is My property. I will give him My property when he becomes an *'abd* to Me. He will not obtain My property unless he becomes My *'abd*. Thus, make him forget what he thinks of as his property. Make him obtain *īmān* in that state. Because I have placed within him the eighteen thousand universes, these sins and karmas have grabbed him, so I must teach him this worship and *'ibādah*. O Muhammad, tell them this!

This *'ilm* has been buried inside the Qur'ān Sharīf. It has not been buried at the depth that people usually study it. It is buried deeper than that. This is why our Nabī Rasūl ☻ has said, "Study *'ilm*, even if you have to go to China." *'Ilm* is extremely heavy. If you want to understand it—if you want to understand the Qur'ān Sharīf—you must study it with people who have more wisdom than you. That is how the Rasūl ☻ has told us to learn.

If you have *īmān*, it is in this state that you need to accept no one other than Allāhu ta'ālā as worthy of worship. We need to realize this. Who is the One worthy of worship? Allāh. You need to firmly accept that there is no God other than Him.

> I am the reason for worship. May they worship Me. If someone looks towards Me once, I will look towards him nine times. If he takes one step towards Me, I will take nine steps towards him. If he thinks of Me once, I will think of him nine times. If he worships Me once, I will do *tasbīh* on his behalf nine times.
>
> O Muhammad, tell them this. It is mutual. If he focuses on Me, I will focus on him; if he thinks of Me, I will think of him; if he worships Me, I will do *tasbīh* on his behalf. If he gives his *salām* and *salawāt* to Me, to the prophets, and to the *aqtāb*, I will give My *salām* to him; I, My prophets, *aqtāb*, and angels will say the *salām* and the *salawāt* to him. Tell them this.
>
> I am his property. He is My property. Thus, he has to give the explanation about Me—as I continually give the explanation about him. Make their *īmān* certain and sure in this state and tell them to accept Me.

> *Yā* Muhammad! Tell them that this is the Kalimah. The strength of he who says the Kalimah with determination is *īmān*. His strength is *īmān*. If he has that strength, I am the One who carries him. Tell them this. I am the Guide. When he realizes with firm conviction that I am his Guide, he will possess nothing other than Me, no wealth other than Me. Everything is Mine. I am the Giver of all things. *Al-hamdu lillāh*. Tell them this. This is the first thing: to strengthen their *īmān*.
>
> Secondly, tell them to worship Me, without the slightest doubt. There is no one worthy of worship except Allāhu ta'ālā. I am the One who is worshipped. Tell this to your *ummah*.

We have lost this. It is because we lost it that the command to give *sadaqah*, charity, was sent down. Allāh told them to give *sadaqah*. The decree came down:

> O Muhammad, tell them to give *sadaqah*. Tell them to give at least five or two or ten out of a hundred. It is My property, and they should not appropriate it. I have increased one seed a thousandfold. The thousandfold increase is not their property. From every seed I give a thousand to a ten thousandfold increase. That is not their property. It is My property. I am making it increase, and increasing the increase. I have increased man, have I not? I increased everything, and increased the increase. That is My property. It is not his property. Tell him to give of it. He has forgotten this. He has forgotten Me. He has forgotten *'ibādah*. He has lost *īmān* and acquired the *dunyā*. Therefore, at least tell them this much.

Because they lost those things, Allāh asked them to fast. This is that fast.

> Tell them to at least realize this fast. The *shart*, the rule, for this fast is to understand the hunger of others and to give to them—to see your own strength wane, to see your own fatigue and exhaustion, and then, out of that understanding, to give something to others; to give food to the hungry, to give clothing to those without clothes. He has usurped their clothing. He has usurped the fruit that was meant for them. He has usurped the *rahmah* of others. Therefore, he must at least realize what he himself experiences, and let that make him help others. Let him give to others. Giving will cure his diseases.
>
> He will clear away his diseases through *wudū'*, ablution, and prayer. Tell him to do ablution and to worship Me. Tell him to do *wudū'* of his *qalb*. We have lost that too. Tell him to complete the hajj. Tell him to dress himself in his shroud and proceed as a corpse. O Muhammad, I decreed this even at the time of Abraham and brought it to completion with you. Thus, tell them to complete the hajj. I brought it to completion through you. Tell them to complete the hajj. Tell them to proceed as a corpse wearing a shroud wound around them just as they wind a shroud around a *mayyit*, the body of a dead person.
>
> Tell them to give away the *mahr*, the mandatory payment, they need to give. Tell them to give to the *miskīn*, the poor person. Tell them to give to their neighbors. After everything has been given away, they have to finish the hajj in a state of death. During this hajj, a person has made the

> *dunyā* a dead thing—his *nafs* are dead, the *dunyā* is dead, his blood ties are dead, his bondage to them is dead. Tell him to make all of his current states dead and then to reach Me. He should at least do this. He needs to at least complete one hajj during his lifetime.

The reason for these explanations of the *furūd* is to dispel those diseases. Through the 6,666 *āyāt*, God has shown us why we must eliminate those illnesses from our *īmān* in every way. He has shown them to us one by one. Not only that but He has shown us that *'ilm* in so many ways through countless *ahādīth*.

It is in this state that we must obtain our freedom on the twenty-seventh day. We must make ourselves clear, do this *wudū'* and *'ibādah*, and then in the place that I described earlier—where we see Allāh as the only Thing that remains—it will be Lailatul-Qadr, where the Light of Nūr Muhammad ☻ comes down.

It comes down into our *īmān* and our *qalb*. The day the Light that shines in our *'ilm*, our love, and our *zīnah*, our beauty, reaches a fully developed state is called Lailatul-Qadr.

It is the twenty-seventh letter, the Light of the *Lām*. The Light of Nūr Muhammad ☻ comes down. *Lām! Alif, Lām, Mīm*.[5] The *Mīm* has overcome so many obstacles in becoming Muhammad ☻. When the *sūrah* of Light known as Muhammad ☻ appears, it means the ray of Light has come down. It means that the Nūr has come down. That Light is called Lailatul-Qadr. It is a day filled with *zīnah*, Light, *'ilm*, *rahmah*. That is the day we call Lailatul-Qadr. We must understand that fast and that *fard*.

If what we are doing now does not cure those illnesses, the Light will not come down. We must cut away those illnesses and understand health and well-being. On the day that our *qalbs* become healthy, the day that we obtain the beauty of the Light

---

5. *Alif, Lām, Mīm*   three letters of the Arabic alphabet, used as mystical letters in the Qur'ān

known as Ahamad[6]—when our *qalb* becomes Ahamad ☻, when the beauty of our countenance becomes Muhammad ☻, on the day the Light known as Nūr Muhammad ☻ comes down—that is the day we will attain well-being, Light, *rahmah*, and perfect purity. That is the twenty-seventh letter, *Lām*, Light, the Light known as Nūr Muhammad ☻.

We must think of this. We need to seek the state in which this state must arise within us. On the day we cut off our connection to earth and to all the eighteen thousand universes, and we see that only Allāh remains, that state of liberation is the liberation known as Lailatul-Qadr.

This is what Allāh and the Rasūl ☻ have told us. These words have been buried within the Qur'ān Sharīf. And there are words that are much deeper. Here we have just told you a little. When you know more, you will understand all of *'ālamul-arwāh* and Allāh's secrets in a way that is even stronger. You must understand this.

It is Lailatul-Qadr today, the twenty-seventh—when you understand the twenty-seventh letter in your *sūrah*, your body, that is Lailatul-Qadr.

When you understand the twenty-eighth letter, that will be the day of your birth, *ammāvāsay*, the time of darkness. That came before. What has to come after darkness is this—the twenty-seventh. Know the day of Light. The day of your birth was Adam ☻, *ammāvāsay*. The day you understand and reach Allāh is Lailatul-Qadr—the day Allāh is understood and purity is attained.

We and you—each child—must know this and understand what kinds of things are the *shart*, the *dunyā*, the ray of Light, and *'ilm*, understanding what kinds of things are health and hygiene, and endeavoring to obtain the liberation described in the Qur'ān Sharīf. We must understand the Light, the liberation, the cutting

---

6. Ahamad ☻ *ahmad* ☻ (Arabic n.) The beauty of the heart that brings beauty to the countenance (*muham,* Tamil n.) is Muhammad ☻, the Messenger of God. That beauty is the beauty of Allāh's qualities. This is a name that comes from within the sea of divine knowledge, *bahrul-'ilm*. Allāh is the One who is worthy of the praise of the heart. Lit. most praiseworthy

away of the diseases, and the *'ilm* of living with happiness. That is our day. *Al-hamdu lillāh.*

Bawa Muhaiyaddeen ☉ immediately proceeds to lead a long dhikr.

Aʿūdhu billāhi minash-shaitānir-rajīm.
I seek refuge in God from the accursed satan.
Bismillāhir-Rahmānir-Rahīm.
In the name of God, the Most Compassionate, the Most Merciful.

THE RAYS OF LIGHT
July 18, 1982

Precious jeweled lights of my eyes, Lailatul-Qadr, the Night of Power, is described in the *ahādīth*, the traditions of the Prophet ☻, and in the Qurʾān as the day the rays of Light descended.

The day the Rasūlullāh ☻ went on *miʿrāj*—the miraculous night journey from Jerusalem to the throne of God—and Lailatul-Qadr are the two days that are described as being very exalted. Therefore we must understand them. They say that of the thirty days of fasting Lailatul-Qadr is the day that the rays of Light descend.

Precious jeweled lights of my eyes, Allāh is a merciful Being, a Being of *rahmah* and Light. He has always been a Being of Light. His Light, His rays of Light, and His *rahmah* descend every second. His *rahmah* is descending even today. That Light descends continuously upon the angels, the truthful, the true human beings, those who are the *Insān Kāmil*, the *ambiyāʾ*, the prophets, the *aqtāb*, those exalted beings sent by Allāh through His grace and mercy, and the people who are the *insān*, the human beings, in the *dunyā* and the *ākhirah,* this world of form and the kingdom of God. The truth is like this. It is through these rays of Light that the destruction of the *dunyā,* all the sections of destruction, are held back. Otherwise, the world would be destroyed because of the sins, because of the karma, because of the separations in the *dunyā*. Destruction is held back because these rays of Light descend upon the good people, the people with *īmān*.

It is said that the month of Ramadān is exalted. However, there is not a second, not a day, not a month, not a *waqt*, not a moment in time, in which Allāhu ta'ālā does not bestow His *rahmah*. Allāh's *rahmah* continuously descends every moment, every second. His *rahmah* descends upon things that are alive and things that are not alive, things that move and things that do not move, things that speak and things that do not speak, things that exist as atoms and all living things, all things that have *hayāh*, life. The weeds, the grasses, the trees, the bushes all contain a sparkle, a light. Without His *rahmah* the taste would not come into a fruit. The sparkle would not come into a weed. The light would not come into a leaf. Because all things contain that spark of Light, that beauty, it means that Allāh's *rahmah* has come down into them.

The Lord who created all things sends down His *rizq*, His sustenance, at each *waqt*, each time. He sends the *rizq*, the water, and the food, does He not? Such a Being who gives like that would also keep sending down His rays of Light. That Light always descends every second, forever. That is why the hunger of His creations stops. The fire of hell that is hunger stops. If that Light did not descend, the fire would not be extinguished. The *rizq* that is His *rahmah* extinguishes the fire.

Thus, the mother of illness, old age, and death is hunger. Illness and old age come from hunger. When hunger comes, the Ten Commandments fly away. When hunger comes, man forgets his sincerity, modesty, restraint, fear of wrongdoing, and faith. The fire of hunger is an immense and cruel fire that exists in all things—a fire that exists in all things God has created.

The fast during the month of Ramadān was decreed because there is a month in which that fire needs to be understood, a month in which that fire needs to be known and a duty needs to be done.

This duty has been decreed so that each person can understand the fire within himself and bring peace to the fire within others. Anyone who owns anything in the *dunyā*, a house in the *dunyā*, or wealth in the *dunyā*, needs to share it with others as well, in order to extinguish the fire of hell. He needs to share and obtain peace.

This is the meaning of having the certitude of the Kalimah, of knowing that there is only one God worthy of worship, that there is nothing other than Allāhu. This is the meaning of saying the Kalimah with certitude and of having *īmān*, of having faith in God.

Second is to have the certitude that everything everywhere belongs only to God. *Insān* belongs to God. Therefore, he must know that there is no other God, no other possession. Only Allāh belongs to him. Allāh is His qualities, His actions, and His conduct. To accept God's merciful qualities, actions, and conduct that are the *rahmah*, to act with those qualities and to worship Him—this is what belongs to *insān*.

On the day man becomes this and does this without any doubt, on the day he attains the absolute faith that his life, his body, his eyes, his nose, his mouth, his ears, his hands, and everything belong to God, he will no longer own anything in the *dunyā* or anywhere else.

He will be absolutely certain that only Allāh belongs to him, and that what belongs to Allāh belongs to everyone.

When fruit grows on a tree, everyone can eat it. The reason God gave the fruit to the tree is that it is for everyone. He gave the leaves to the tree for everyone. He grows things in the earth for everyone so that they can share those things and eat them. Similarly, he who is *insān* will understand the fire of hunger in himself, knowing that it also exists in others, and bring peace to others by putting out that fire. If his *niyyah*, his intention, and his qualities are correct, he will put out that fire. He will extinguish the fire that burns in all stomachs.

It is because we did not properly strengthen our *īmān*, because we did not properly accept Allāh's words, that these three *furūd*, these three obligatory duties, were sent down: *sadaqah*, or charity; fasting; and hajj, or pilgrimage. This is why we speak of fasting during the month of Ramadān.

Those who came before us also fasted. Fasting has been decreed since the time of Adam ☻. The five obligatory duties came at that time. Because the people did not become aware, charity, fasting, and hajj were clearly explained at the end to Muhammad ☻. "You must perform these *furūd*—these duties are obligatory." Fasting came so that we could be aware of our obligatory duties. This is the reason for the fast.

When we correctly perform the obligatory duties, when we are ready to extinguish the fire of hunger in others, the cruel fire of the sorrows and suffering and illness of others, when we give clothing as charity so that others can safeguard their modesty, when that *niyyah*, that intention, and those qualities come to us, it is then that we will complete the fast every day. We will be fasting every second with "*Lā ilāha illAllāh.*" That will benefit us. Every day, every second, every moment there are so many kinds of fasting that take place just like the fast that takes place during the month of Ramadān. There are so many kinds of fasts.

We must be aware of the reasons for the fast. Even if you do not or cannot fast, you must know that the reason for the fast is to realize that we must extinguish the fire in others at least during this time. He who is *insān* needs to correctly understand this *fard*.

If he gains a clear understanding of this explanation, he will be a person who will be in *'ibādah*, a state of worship and duty to God, a person with God's qualities, a person who does God's duty without fail in order to extinguish the fire of hell in others. He will be a person who is able to extinguish the fire of the *qalb*, the fire of the stomach, the fire of the *nafs*, the fire of desire, the fire of maya, the fire of the hypnotic delusions, and the fire of *shaitān*. He will be a person who can extinguish all these fires in himself, in others, in his brothers and sisters, in his neighbors, in all who have been born with him, in his parents, in his children, in everyone. He will be a person who can extinguish the fires and bring peace.

He will complete the fast during his lifetime on the day he can be aware of that with certitude and do that duty. Then he will complete the fast. He will obtain the reward on that day.

He does not complete the fast until he does that duty. Until then, we are just doing what the world is doing. Until the completion arrives, until the ray of Light descends, we cannot obtain the reward. When a human being fulfills the fast correctly, the ray of Light will come down upon him. The Light of Allāh, the *rahmah* of Allāh, and the wealth of Allāh's *mubārakāt*—the wealth of grace, the wealth of meaning, the wealth of the soul, the wealth of wisdom, the wealth of *'ilm*, and the wealth of Allāh's qualities will come down upon him.

This is Lailatul-Qadr, the Night of Power. Allāh's beauty and Light will be visible in that human being. Allāh's qualities and actions will be visible in him—Allāh's qualities and actions will be in his *'ilm*, and the *rahmah* of Allāh will emerge from him. Everything that emerges from him will bring peace to all lives. This day is Lailatul-Qadr.

In days long gone by, only one person each year would successfully complete the hajj. The Light would come down once a year upon one person. Similarly, the ray of Light will come down upon the one who realizes this and acts accordingly. If there is at least one person in the *dunyā* who attains this state, the ray of Light will come down upon him. Just as the *rahmah* of Allāh would come down once a year to one person during hajj, the ray of Light would come down upon one person in this state.

That is what is protecting the *dunyā* today, a place where there would otherwise be so many more difficulties. Without that, the *dunyā* would perish. It would burn in the fire. The *dunyā* would burn in the fire, in the evil qualities of the people. The people would burn.

It is said that this ray of Light comes down on one day, but it comes down every day. Because we do not understand, because we do not know, we have made only this month exalted. So at least become aware during this month!

Precious jeweled lights of my eyes, the day this ray of Light descends, our fire will be extinguished, the fires of many people will be extinguished, the needs of many people will be fulfilled. However, it is Allāhu ta'ālā Nāyan who extinguishes all the fires at every moment through His gracious blessings.

Even though Allāh ends the hunger of the stomach, even though He extinguishes the fire of the stomach, the fire still burns in the mind of *insān*. The fire is in his mind. The hunger is in his mind. There is not nearly as much hunger in the stomach as there is in the mind. The hunger in the mind is the hunger of the *nafs*, the self. No matter how much wealth *insān* amasses, his hunger does not cease. He will not give to others. He will not allow himself to be aware that others are starving—he will not give to others.

His hunger never ends. No matter how much *rahmah* God gives him, if one of his neighbors possesses an atom of something, he will attempt to take even that atom from him. He will attempt to seize it for himself. Such is his hunger! Whether it is his neighbors or other people, if they have an atom of something, he will still try to gain possession of that atom—even if he himself has shiploads of wealth. Such is the hunger of the mind! It is a hunger that will never end.

The animals seek food for their one-span stomachs and their hunger stops. They seek food for their hunger. All created beings seek food when they are hungry. When that fire comes, they find something to eat and say *al-hamdu lillāh*, all praise belongs to God.

Only man does not search purely for the hunger of his stomach. He searches for what his *nafs* tell him, for what his mind shows him. The hunger of the mind will never end. His hunger will not end in hell, in the day or in the night, when he is asleep or when he is awake, in profit or in loss. He will never control that hunger even on the day of his death.

Allāhu ta'ālā Nāyan has decreed this month of Ramadān for the person who possesses this kind of hunger, for a person whose mind is hungry. He has told us to feed the hungry, to extinguish the fire in the stomachs of those who are hungry. He has demonstrated this by decreeing the month of Ramadān to be a month of fasting. He has said, "I have given *rahmah* to you as I have given fruit to a tree. Share it with everyone."

The Rasūl ☉ has demonstrated this to us in his actions and his demeanor. However, man did not realize what he was being shown. He did not act accordingly. The fast was sent down just as each *āyah*, each verse, of the Qur'ān was sent down. The 6,666 *āyāt* were sent down for specific reasons. There are countless *ahādīth* that came down for specific reasons.

We must think of this during our lives. Day and night we must think of how to end the hunger of others, the illness of others, the suffering of others. When the thought of *shukūr*, gratitude, comes to us when we are hungry, when we tie the stone of *īmān*, *sabūr*, and *shukūr*, faith, patience, and gratitude, to our own stomach for the sake of the hunger of others and share the food that we have with others who are hungry, *that* is the day we will be fasting.

Such a person will be completing the fast every second. His fast will be kept according to his intention. He will obtain the *rahmah*. The Light will appear within him. The *rahmah* will pour down upon him endlessly. The Light will come down upon him. The Light of Allāh and the blessing of Allāh will come down upon him every day.

The qualities, the *rahmah*, and the blessings of Allāh will come down upon him every day and alert him to do more.

The eye of Allāh's grace will look upon him every day and protect him. God's protection will be with him day and night. Allāh will protect him. Just as such a person is aware of others and just as he safeguards others, Allāh will safeguard him. That day is Lailatul-Qadr. That *waqt* is Lailatul-Qadr.

Every day that *insān* receives this reward is an exalted day. We say that the month of Ramadān is an exalted month. For a person of wisdom, every day that he shares with others the *rahmah* that he has been given is an exalted day for him.

A person whose wisdom has not fully blossomed should at least become aware of these things during this month. That will be a good time for him. If he can do this for at least one month out of the year, it will bring him a reward in his life.

Islām is not something that gives because someone is begging for alms. It is something in which you must give all of yourself. Islām does not wait for a hungry person to ask for food. A Muslim looks at another person's face and his state to see if he is hungry. He looks at such a person's house and finds that person so he can give to him. This is the meaning. This is Islām.

Islām is the section of *sabūr*. There is no begging in Islām. It is not very good to give charity to someone who has to beg for it. To give five cents or ten cents to someone who is begging—to get change for one rupee and distribute it to ten people, to give out five or twenty cents at a time to beggars—this is not Islām! This is not the *hadīyah*, the gift, that Islām gives.

Hadīyah means to dedicate oneself, to offer oneself as the gift. In days long gone by, *hadīyah* meant to give one's own *rūh*, one's own soul, to Allāh while giving one's own body to the people as a gift. Such a person gives away his own well-being so that others can be well.

Similarly, *hadīyah* means to give so that poverty-stricken young girls can afford to be married, to give to women without husbands, to give to orphans, children who do not have mothers or fathers. A wealthy man should look around the entire region to see what is needed. He should give anonymously, wherever the need exists, to help the people find peace. This is Īmān-Islām. This is the *fard* of Islām.

Some people go begging from house to house because of the pain of hunger. Some people make begging their occupation. Currently in Islām, there are a few who are wealthy and many who are forced to beg. It is not enough to give ten cents to a beggar! You must search out people who are in need, give to them, and make them peaceful. To bring this state into action is the meaning of Islām. We must realize this. We must do this for as long as we are alive.

Begging does not exist in Islām. If there is food in one house, there is food in all the houses. If there is starvation in one house, there is starvation in all the houses. If there is a funeral in one house, there is a funeral in all the houses. If there is sadness in one house, there is sadness in all the houses. If there is sorrow in one house, there is sorrow in all the houses. If there is happiness in one house, there is happiness in all the houses. This is Islām.

The day that this state arises in Islām is the day that Islām will be pure and holy. This will be heaven, Allāh's kingdom. We who are *insān* must realize this. Islām is purity.

Although there are four scriptures, az-Zabūr, al-Jabbūrat, al-Injīl, and al-Furqān, he who accepts Allāh will accept the truth. He will accept goodness. We are the children of Adam ☺. Allāh is One. Truth is one. Prayer is one. We are one family. Anyone who understands this truth and who obtains Allāh's qualities, who acts with Allāh's actions, who makes peace, who regards the lives of others as his own life, and who acts with Allāh's qualities is a person of purity. Such a person is a Muslim—Islām means purity.

He who helps another who is suffering, he who helps another who is in pain, he who helps another who is hungry is a Muslim. He can be called a Muslim. He who brings another person to his own state of peace is a Muslim. He who experiences the pain of another as his own pain is a Muslim. Allāh will bless anyone who thinks these kinds of good thoughts. This is Islām.

Islām has no bigotry. Islām has no differences, no separations, no enmities, no fights, no arguments, no jealousies, no envy, no vengeance. Islām does not say, "She is different, he is different." The enemy of Islām is evil qualities—*shaitān's* qualities. That is the enemy. *Shaitān* means evil qualities. The qualities that harm others are *shaitān's* qualities—they are ignorant qualities. They are the qualities that separate us from Allāh, the qualities that separate us from goodness, the qualities that turn us away from truth. That is *shaitān*. It is *shaitān* alone who is the enemy to truth. Those qualities are *shaitān*.

Shaitān will come to you if you have those qualities. He will come if you have falsehood. He will come if you have envy. He will come if you have doubt. He will come if you backbite. He will come if you have deceit and treachery. Those evil qualities are *shaitān*. Those are his treasures. That is *shaitān*.

Īmān-Islām exists to transform those qualities. Anyone who transforms those qualities will be transforming hell and *shaitān*. He will be transforming the *adhāb*, the punishment, the questions in the grave, and the Day of Judgment. This is Islām.

Fasting, *sadaqah*, and hajj are all related to this. Brothers and sisters, we must think of this. If you can change your state, that Light will come down upon you. Lailatul-Qadr refers to the moment the ray of Allāh's Light descends, the day that Allāh's qualities, His ray of Light, and His beauty come down upon us.

On that day we can become *mu'minūn*. Then we will understand *Insān Kāmil*, *mu'min*, and Islām. We must think of this and act accordingly. Precious jeweled lights of my eyes, if each child could think of this, if we could think of our lives and the lives of others, and if we could act accordingly, we would focus on Allāh at every moment.

We would pray to Him, we would worship Him, we would do *tasbīh* to Him in every breath. We would do *taubah*, we would ask forgiveness, at every moment. We would block every thought of doing evil to someone who has harmed us. We would do *taubah* for our own mistakes. If we were to feel vengeful—because Islām does not harbor jealousy or vengeance—we would forget any harm done to us the very moment it was done. That is Islām. To forget it that very second is Islām.

To be peaceful and tranquil is Islām. When this state arises, the *rahmah* of the hajj of old will come down upon you. Allāh will declare your state complete. Anyone who attains this state has completed the hajj. The hajj that comes once a year will be completed.

The ray of Light that is known as Lailatul-Qadr will come down upon anyone who completes this state. Anyone who changes his *qalb* like this and does this kind of duty will become a *mu'min*, a believer. Such people will know the answers to the questions, their death, the Day of Qiyāmah here itself, and obtain their reward.

We must be aware of this. This was what was called fasting in the days of old.

We must understand the inner meaning of fasting. If we understand and if we perform those duties, the ray of Light that is Allāh's *rahmah* will come down upon us—the beauty, the Light, and the *rahmah* will come down upon us without end.

On that day, such a person will be an *insān* who is a *mu'min*.

We must understand this. Precious jeweled lights of my eyes, please understand this. As long as we live, we must endeavor to discern each duty we have to do. This is the duty that those who are the *mu'minūn* will do.

The evil qualities are *shaitān's* qualities, the evil qualities that were cursed by Allāh. Our good qualities have been made to appear from within Allāh. Good qualities have been commanded for us. That is why there is hell for evil qualities and Allāh's kingdom for good qualities. We must do those good duties. We must transform the qualities that conceal the truth from us, nurture unity, and bring peace to others.

May Allāh fulfill our intentions.

Because it is time for you to break your fast, we will stop here now. *Āmīn. As-salāmu 'alaikum wa rahmatullāhi wa barakātuhu.*

May Allāh fulfill your intentions. May Allāh fulfill your *niyyah*. May He accept your fast and bestow His blessing, His *rahmah,* and His grace upon you. May He transform any illnesses, or diseases, or harmful conditions, or *shaitān's* qualities that could come to you in the inner realm and in the outer realm. May He bless you with good actions and good *rahmah*.

May He heal all the diseases of the body, the diseases of the eyes, the diseases of the ears, the diseases of the nose, the diseases of the mind—all the diseases that could arise from the body.

May you be given the good gift of Allāh's *rahmah*, the wealth of the *mubārakāt*. May He feed you with the milk of grace and honey, the milk of wisdom, the milk of His *qudrah*, His power. May He raise you at the breast of His *rahmah*.

Āmīn. Āmīn. May He pardon all our mistakes, and forgive us. *Āmīn. As-salāmu 'alaikum wa rahmatullāhi wa barakātuhu.*

Bismillāhir-Rahmānir-Rahīm. Break your fast. Allāh is sufficient. May He fulfill your intentions.

A'ūdhu billāhi minash-shaitānir-rajīm.
I seek refuge in God from the accursed satan.
Bismillāhir-Rahmānir-Rahīm.
In the name of God, the Most Compassionate, the Most Merciful.

THE STATE OF READINESS
July 7, 1983

Bismillāhir-Rahmānir-Rahīm. The state of the One who is the Giver of Immeasureable Grace, the One who is Incomparable Love, the Rabbal-'ālamīn, the Lord and Cherisher of all the universes, bestows upon us inexhaustible wealth in our lives through the service that we do, through the duties that we do for Him with our qualities, actions, and conduct, through the duties that we do for the people and for other lives.

The blessings we get from doing those duties are the wealth— they will become the completion of our wealth in the *dunyā* and the *ākhirah*, jeweled lights of my eyes.

The timing of the blessings we could receive were indicated to humankind by the *najjām,* the ancient astronomers, on the day, on the week, on the month, or on the year that certain prophets appeared. This exists in many ways. There is not just one time— there are many times, many days, many nights, many weeks, many months, many years that have been pointed out to us, indicating that it was the time that a significant benediction would be sent down.

Precious jeweled lights of my eyes, this is what the *ambiyā'* came to remind us of. The divine messengers of Allāh and the *auliyā'* have come since the time of Adam ☺ until now. After the Rasūl ☺ came as the Last Nabī ☺, the *auliyā'*, the *aqtāb*, the *gnānis*, and the guides came as His representatives in the *dunyā*. God sent them down.

Through them, Allāh explained certain things about good and evil, destruction and construction. After the *ambiyā'*, God sent down the *auliyā'*, the people of wisdom, and the *aqtāb* in each time to disseminate good thoughts, good conduct, wisdom, and understanding.

Even though we can no longer see the *ambiyā'* and the *auliyā'* with our eyes, for our wisdom and for our *qalbs* there is a unity with their integrity and an ability to see them. If we look for them with our *qalbs* and our wisdom, they will be close to us in that state. God will keep them close to us. This is certain.

For anything beneficial we seek, if our *qalbs* and our wisdom search together in a state of harmony, God will bring what we seek close to us and unite us with it. Thus, it is through this that the *rahmah*, the great wealth we seek, will be abundantly given to us.

Because God is the Bestower of all good blessings, He will give you everything you want. He is the Bestower of all good blessings.

Precious jeweled lights of my eyes. We have to be prepared. We have to be prepared in all situations and circumstances. God is prepared. He does not possess the work of the *dunyā*, the *nafs*, desire, and selfishness. He does His duty—the work He does equally for everyone—holding all lives within Himself as His own life. He does His duty and serves all lives because He holds everything within Himself. He has no outer work. He has no selfishness, so the only work He has is for the people. That is why it is easy for Him.

However, we the children of Adam ☉ have selfish work that we do for ourselves. We have *self-business*, our own work. We have the *dunyā*, our wife and children, our home and property, our cattle and goats, our possessions and well-being, our fame and titles, our celebrity and honors, our jobs, praise and blame, hells and heavens, truths and falsehoods. We have taken possession of those and similar things.

Because of this possessive state, we are not prepared to relinquish any of them. The moment we let go of one thing, another will come to grab us. Thus, we are never ready. We are not ready for God's readiness.

It is because we were not prepared that every *nabī*, every

prophet, brought each instruction, gradually giving us wisdom, understanding, and God's qualities, telling us, "Be prepared! Be ready! Reject this! Reject that! Accept this! Do that! Gather this!" God was doing this work to prepare us.

We must be like Him. He is ready at all times to help us. We are not ready. That is the difficulty facing us. He is giving us His hand, but we are not ready. We are looking over here for work, we are looking over there for work. We are looking at one thing or another.

It is because we were never ready that God very gradually sent us worship, the five daily prayers, *'ibādah*, *dhikr*, *fikr*, good qualities, good actions, good deeds, good thoughts, modesty, sincerity, reserve, fear of wrongdoing, good conduct, goodness, surrender, concentration, balance, *gnānam*, love, patience, *sabūr*, *shukūr*, *tawakkul*, *al-hamdu lillāh*, justice, conscience, unity, peace, compassion, mercy, and the ninety-nine actions and deeds of God, the *wilāyāt*.

The *ambiyā'* and the *auliyā'*, the prophets and the saints, came to show us these things and when we did as they instructed, they said to us, "Avoid what is wrong. Our wealth is the one wealth. It is the treasure that is certain and inexhaustible. It is the wealth of the soul, the wealth of the *ākhirah*, the treasure of our lives, the house for our life—paradise."

The treasures within it are inexhaustible. The wealth for the soul is made up of the treasures of the *'ilm*, the treasures of wisdom, the treasures of compassion and good qualities. We must be ready to obtain them. We must be ready to accept God's commonwealth.

If we prepare ourselves just as He prepared Himself, we will be ready at all times. We will always be prepared. Then we will always be ready to make requests of Him and to have those requests granted.

However, when we are in our state and He calls us, we have work!

We say, "I can't leave my child. I can't leave my land. I can't leave my horse. I can't leave my donkey. Wait a little! I will finish this work and then come to You. Wait until I finish this work. Wait, I have to give the child milk. Wait, I have to polish this first. Wait, I have to get my shoes. Wait, I have to put socks on this child."

We have too much work. He is holding out His hand, looking for us, carrying us. He is ready. He is ready for us at all times. He is ready to accept us, to give to us, to embrace us, and to carry us. We are not ready.

That is why God sent down the 124,000 prophets—to get us ready. From among them, He selected twenty-five prophets and made them clear, sending them down to explain the ancient histories and epics as paths and ways.

Among them, He made eight prophets even more clear. He bestowed upon them the ability to perform miracles and wonders. He told them to show these to the people and gave them teachings of wisdom so they could give the people good explanations.

However, we did not obtain liberation or freedom through those teachings. We were not ready to free ourselves from enslavement. So they said, "At least then, worship, do the five daily prayers, do ʿibādah, dhikr, and fikr. Believe in Him, worship Him, give sadaqah to the poor. Or else fast in order to realize how you feel when you are hungry and then serve others when they are hungry."

Think: *If poverty were to come to us, how difficult it would be for the children. If we had no money or resources, the children would starve and cry.* Have you not heard your neighbors' children crying? Have you not seen the suffering that comes from poverty and starvation? When hunger comes, the Ten Commandments will fly away. The faith of starving people will depart. Hunger makes you forget everything—your faith, your caste, your family, and your community, does it not? Wisdom and the Ten Commandments will depart. You must realize this.

With regard to hunger, you must love your neighbors as yourself. You should look at their hunger, their faces, their stomachs, and give them rice. You should give them some of what you have and make them peaceful.

It is *dāna-darumam*, charitable giving, to give clothing to someone who has no clothing, to safeguard his modesty. If you have nothing else, you should give him half of your clothing. Even if you have only one garment, you should tear off a piece of that garment so he can safeguard his modesty, saying, "This is all I have. Here, this is for you." You should at least give him what amounts to a loincloth to safeguard his modesty.

Dāna-darumam is charitable giving. We must give our hearts and give from what we have. To give someone clothing is to preserve their modesty. If necessary, we have to give them some of what we are wearing. We are not doing that. We have not realized that.

At the very least, we should realize that the hunger of others is like our own and give to them. When hunger comes, the Ten Commandments fly away. His wisdom will depart. When hunger torments him, he will lose the truth, he will lose his integrity, he will steal, he will lie, he will attempt to kill. Therefore, we must realize that.

We must help everyone just as we help our neighbors, our relatives, our parents, and our friends. Others get hungry just as we do. You must give them some of your own food. Help them. Help the poor. You may have grown rich by taking something that belonged to them. Thus, give them back some of the property they gave you.

God has created the earth and everything else as a commonwealth that belongs equally to everyone, but some of you took more and grew wealthier.

God created the fruit and the trees with equality. Perhaps you took four more trees than you should have. Perhaps you became rich because you took more than your share. Thus you must give back the portion that rightfully belongs to others. Give them their share and make them peaceful. That is why Allāh sent down the prophets—to show us each reason for doing these things.

This is why we fast. Yet, if we do not care for the lives of others, if we do not understand their hunger, their thirst, or their illness, what is the benefit of fasting for a thousand years? If for a thousand years we do not understand the hunger and poverty of others or help them, what benefit will we receive from the things we accumulate? What benefit will we get from our worship? We would be sinners!

The very least we can do is to understand what it feels like to fast.

If we do not understand how the hunger of others squeezes them just as it squeezes us, how they undergo the hardship of poverty, then we should at least go on hajj, on pilgrimage. We know that people can die while traveling to distant mosques. The fifth *fard* is to proceed in the state of death. If you have not given *sadaqah*, if you have not fasted, then you must go on hajj and give away your possessions: a portion for your wife; a portion for the children; a portion for the poor; a portion for your neighbors; and so forth. You must complete the hajj in a state of death. That is called the fifth *fard*.

The fifth *fard* is that the *dunyā* is *maut*—the world is dead—for you. As you proceed, the *dunyā* must die within you. You must become *hayāh* to the *ākhirah* but *maut* to the *dunyā*—alive to the kingdom of God but dead to the world.

This is the journey. You are journeying to reach Him. You are leaving the world. You must establish this state. These are the five *furūd*.

There are five daily prayers, five *furūd*, five duties, and Friday is the fifth weekday. We die on a certain day, just as we are born on a certain day. We are born on Monday and we disappear into Him on Friday. This is how we are born and how we die. On Friday, we disappear into Allāh, into worship. On Sunday, we must dedicate the creations, the *dunyā*, our bodies, and opinions to Him. Then on the Monday that is *'ālamul-arwāh*, the world of pure souls, we must be born in Allāh.

If we can do this each week, our lives will be made clear.

Precious jeweled lights of my eyes, each thing that we do like this has been done by the prophets and the saints. What will come from these practices is Light—luminous rays of Light, resplendence, *gnānam*, the radiance of *gnānam*, rays of *gnānam*, His *wahy*, His *'ilm*, His perfection. There are a hundred kinds of rays emerging from His *wilāyāt* that have been made to descend as three thousand kinds of grace.

In prayer, there are three thousand kinds of grace. When we act with His qualities, He gives us three thousand kinds of grace. God sends them down to us. Three thousand kinds of grace descend as resplendences. As each resplendence comes to each of our limbs, each of our faculties, we feel them as flames, but they exist as resplendences. In that prayer, the prayer for His intention, there are ninety-nine *wilāyāt* through which Allāh sends down His great Light.

As a result of what we do, Allāhu ta'ālā sends His ninety-nine *wilāyāt* as a precious essence, as Light, as rays of Light, as resplendence, as grace, as *gnānam*, as *'ilm*, and as His beautiful deeds. Everything is radiant with rays of Light, resplendent, perfect *'ilm*, wisdom, *gnānam*, and understanding. In this state these are the qualities of peace that come as resplendent Lights. These Lights come to us as our wealth, our completion.

It has been said that today is Lailatul-Qadr, the Night of Power, the twenty-seventh day of the fast, the day on which those rays appear.

It has been said that a Light will be sent down as a reward for the good we have done, that today, through God, the Light is sent down according to how we have fasted. Just as the Light of God may descend upon only one of thousands of people who go on hajj, God's Light may descend only upon one of thousands of people who are fasting. It will descend upon those who are in this state. Such is His *qudrah*, His power.

Like this, God's *qudrah* and His *rahmah* will descend upon the one person out of thousands who correctly completes the fast, depending upon his state. This is the day that it occurs—Lailatul-Qadr—the twenty-seventh day.

The twenty-eighth day [of the lunar month] is *ammāvāsay*, the dark night [when there is no moon]. Tonight is the last night—the fast ends tomorrow. There will be no moon tomorrow night. Thus, today is the day we can obtain completion, the day we can become complete. Today, our prayers will be completed. Today is the day the Light of God is born.

For three days after the dark night—the first crescent comes, then the second crescent, and the third crescent. *Ammāvāsay* is dark. The day after that is the day the *gnānis* see the crescent moon—the day the *malā'ikah* and the *gnānis* see the crescent moon illuminating the darkness of the world.

Angels and *gnānis* in the *ākhirah* can see in the dark—in the darkness of the *dunyā*. The *ākhirah* is always bright with Light. Truth is always bright. *'Ilm* is always bright. The Light is always bright. Truth, the *ākhirah*, Rabbul-'ālamīn, the Lord of the Universes, *gnānam*, Light, and *'ilm* are always bright.

Only the *dunyā* is dark. Only the *dunyā* contains the *ammāvāsay*, and this is so the darkness and the Light can be revealed.

He who dies before death has no darkness. He has no darkness! He who has no darkness has no age. How can his age be counted? It is only when the darkness and the daylight appear in progression that we can count time: "This is today and that is tomorrow." Without darkness, he who dies before death has only one day. How can his age be calculated?

Similarly, when wisdom comes to someone, when Allāh's *qudrah* and *'ilm* come to such a person, when God's qualities and actions come to him, he will have no age and no darkness, no dusk and no dawn. He will have ever-present, everlasting Light. He will have no age and no darkness. So many tens and tens of millions of years will go by in the *dunyā*, but not for him. The years will go by for the earth, the darkness will come, the hours will come, the seasons will come, but truth will never age. *Gnānam* will never age. Allāh will never age. Honesty will never age. Wisdom will never age. The soul will never age. The Light is within them.

It is the same for us. For our seasons, for our age, becoming *maut*, dead, and becoming *hayāh*, alive, occur because of the things we hold within ourselves. As long as we have darkness we have death.

Youth is the time of dispelling the darkness, the time of Light, the Light of the soul, life, God. *Hayāh* is the time of Light, the time without *maut*.

These times are the times we obtain the *kadir oli*, the rays of Light. The rays of Light are sent down through the *qudrah* of God upon what we have done during many days. That is why it is called Lailatul-Qadr—the Light that comes from the rays God has sent down. That is the *rahmah*, the grace, we receive.

This reward comes from God because of the meditations we perform, the duties we do, the fasts we undertake, the prayers that we pray. This reward is a flawless, limitless reward.

For our life, for our journey, for our existence, these rays of Light are the *daulat*, the greatest wealth. We have to experience hardship in order to obtain this great wealth. The reward we obtain from it will be the happiness, the bliss, the fullness of heart, the blossoming fragrance of the *qalb*, its beauty and delight. Precious jeweled lights of my eyes, each child, we must think. Yet, no matter how much we think and think of this in our lives, our goal is to complete this task, and through it to reach and obtain the reward. That is why we have come here as *insān*, as human beings.

Precious jeweled lights of my eyes, people speak of the five daily prayers. The first is the connection to earth. That is the *subh* prayer. In this prayer, we understand the connection to earth and we take what is correct in it. We cut that connection during the *subh* prayer. In the earth is the *rahmah* of Allāh known as Adam ☺ who was created of earth by God, was he not? God pressed the Light known as Nūr Muhammad ☺ into the forehead of Adam ☺, and sent the *rūh* down into him. He pressed into his forehead *gnānam*, the *'ilm* of *gnānam*, and His own Light. Within that, He sent down His ray of Light. That is the *rūh*, the soul. In the prayer of *subh*, we renounce the earth and we accept the Light of wisdom. At *subh* we need to cut our connection to earth.

The second is the prayer of *zuhr*. The air flows throughout the body as breath. The section that arises through breathing is that of the two breaths, one running on the left, the other running on the right. Fire and air come with the breath. The *nafs*, hunger, and sin come with it. We must understand this *waqt*, this time, of prayer, see what the section of the air is like, and renounce it. We must cut into it and take in the air of the Light of the soul to God's section.

The third is the prayer of *'asr*. *'Asr* is the heart, a soft pouch of water where air and water intermingle. Because air and water are within us in the lungs and in the heart, they are connected to us. Those three elements are connected. We must know this as we cut away these connections to the air.

Earth, fire, water, and air! We must endeavor to cut away our connections to them.

The fourth is *maghrib*. We must endeavor to cut away our connection to death, our bondage to kinship, earth, and so forth. *Maghrib* is for bringing about the death of this section in the body. We must endeavor to cut away our bondage to kinship and make it die.

The fifth is *'ishā'*. The *waqt* of *'ishā'* comes at night. What is the state of our dying before death? All of our desires must be put to rest. We must understand how the body is made to die, how the soul is transformed into Light, how the loan is repaid—we must give the loan of the body back to God's responsibility.

That is the day we will see Allāhu as the only One that remains. To see Him as all that remains, we must return to Him the treasure He loaned us. We accepted and experienced His treasure, and now we must return it to Him. We must establish that state during the fifth prayer.

If we understand these five duties like this, the *dunyā* will die. Renouncing the five elements and making the *dunyā* die will bring our life back to life—our *hayāh* will become *hayāh*. We will form a connection to Allāh. Only His treasure will remain. Everything else will be dead. That will be dying before death. We will have died before death, we will have repaid the loans, we will have cut away the connections. Now we have died before death. Now we have the treasure that will never die. Now all the things that need to die have died. We have to think of these things.

Precious jeweled lights of my eyes, we speak of *vanakkam*, worship. *Vanakkam* means to be ready. *Vanakkam* means that the appropriate state of readiness needs to exist between ourselves and Allāh. There is no one worthy of worship other than Allāhu ta'ālā Nāyan. When there is no other Nāyan, no other Lord or Master, when there is only One God, when the readiness between Him and our *qalbs* is made complete, *that* is readiness. To structure this in the correct way is *vanakkam*. First there is *vanakkam* and then there is *'ibādah*, when we place our intention in His responsibility. First we must make our intention and worship ready. There must be a connection between God and our *qalbs*. Our intention must be given into His responsibility.

First there is *vanakkam* and then there is *'ibādah*. Our *'ibādah* must be placed in His responsibility and connected to Him. Our *niyyah*, our intention, and our focus must be placed in His responsibility. We must let them form within Him.

Toluhay, prayer, occurs when we go to Him and surrender into Him. *Rukū'*, the bow in prayer, means to become an *'abd*, a slave, to Him. *Toluhay* is surrender. To perform the *rukū'* means to put your head on His feet and to become His slave, saying, "Accept me, fully accept me!" To dissolve into Him is *toluhay* and *vanakkam*.

Dhikr is to dissolve the self and to speak the words that exist between the *qalb* and God through the breath that flows without flowing, through the speech that communes without speech. *Dhikr* is the speech spoken between the *qalb* and God with neither speech nor breath. This speech is merged with the *rūh*, the soul. This intention, this focus, this speech exists within God every second.

The intention is the speech. The intention, the thought, the idea, the word, the *sindanay*, is the speech that we speak with Him. It is the never-to-be-forgotten *sindanay*, the remembrance of how we once existed with God in the world of pure souls.

If we can establish these in the correct way, this state is Lailatul-Qadr. This is what descends as the reward for what we do.

Today is Friday eve, the twenty-seventh day of the fast in which that ray of Light descends. Allāh causes it to be sent down from His *'arsh*, His throne, to His children, to their *qalbs*. He sends it down into the *'ilm* in their *qalbs*, into the knowledge of the divine in their hearts. God is ready to fully accept His children. We must be clearly ready to accept Him. If we rise up, we can obtain that opportunity.

Precious jeweled lights of my eyes, today is the twenty-seventh day of the fast, called Lailatul-Qadr, the Night of Power, the day in which we can obtain the reward. Tonight, people do *tasbīh* to God until morning. They do *dhikr* to God. They say the *salām* and the *salawāt*. They recite the Qur'ān. They speak about the prophets. They recite the *ahādīth*. Some people do this until morning.

Some people go to the cinema. Some people go to the dance hall. Some people stay in the mosque. Some people may express their love of God outside of the mosque. Some may be alone. Some may sit in groups in the mosques, speaking of many things. Some may pray and then tell a *hadīth* every half hour, and read the Qur'ān. They may stay in prayer like this tonight. These are the kinds of things they may do tonight, the night they say the reward is received.

I do not know. I do not know whether anyone has received the reward or not. I have just heard people talking like that. God has to help us. Each person will know for himself what he receives on this day. We are happy, no matter to whom Allāh gives this. We are happy if He gives it to everyone and everything is good.

However, Allāh has to look at us a little and protect and help us too. We do not know *'ilm*. We have not studied. We do not know what *vanakkam* is. We do not know what prayers are. We are just shouting here as we proceed on our way. But God knows our path. He also has to protect those who do not know. He has to grant them grace and patience.

With *sabūr* and *shukūr*, we have to say, "*Yā* Rahmān, please help us. That is Your responsibility. You have to safeguard and forgive those who do not know. You have to show us the good path and help us. That is our prayer.

"You must open the way for us. We have too much work! If only You could slightly reduce our work, in the way You have reduced it for others. We have work to do! That is why we are not ready. Make us ready. If You could make us ready, and bestow Your wealth upon us, O Rahmān, it would be good. *Al-hamdu lillāh*.

"We are practicing *shukūr*, O Rahmān! But You have the *shukūr* and we do not. We do not have anything. Bless us with *shukūr*. Do this, guide us to the straight path, and give us the grace.

"Now it is time. *Al-hamdu lillāh*. *Yā* Rabbal-'ālamīn, O Lord and Cherisher of all the Universes. All praise belongs to You. Now it is time to break the fast. It is time. They have to say the call to prayer, end their fast, and do their duties. Please forgive us."

We will stop now to break the fast. *Al-hamdu lillāh*. *As-salāmu 'alaikum wa rahmatullāh*.

Salawāt *for the Prophet Muhammad* ☺.

Āmīn. As-salāmu 'alaikum wa rahmatullāhi wa barakātuhu.

A'ūdhu billāhi minash-shaitānir-rajīm.
I seek refuge in God from the accursed satan.
Bismillāhir-Rahmānir-Rahīm.
In the name of God, the Most Compassionate, the Most Merciful.

Heaven Is the Reward
June 26, 1984

A'ūdhu billāhi minash-shaitānir-rajīm. I seek refuge in God from the accursed satan. *Bismillāhir-Rahmānir-Rahīm.* In the name of God, the Most Compassionate, the Most Merciful.

May all praise and glory be to Allāh. May He bestow upon us His blessing, the treasures of His *mubārakāt*, His blessed qualities, His *rahmah*, His beautiful qualities. May all our praise be to Him. May Allāhu ta'ālā Nāyan bestow upon us His qualities, actions, and rewards. May we obtain those treasures.

May we obtain the treasures of His *mubārakāt* and attain peace, tranquility, and harmony. May we obtain peace in God's kingdom, the world's kingdom, and the heavenly kingdom; in the kingdoms of the *awwal* and the *ākhirah*, in the kingdom of the *rūh*, the soul, and in the kingdom of the *dunyā*—in all three worlds. May we obtain peace for the soul, peace for the *rūh*, peace in the life of the *dunyā*, the world, peace in attaining liberation for the soul, and peace in the *ākhirah*. May we obtain that peace and exist in peace and tranquility. May Allāhu ta'ālā Nāyan bestow that blessing upon us with His grace. May we obtain His *mubārakāt* and always live in peace.

Precious jeweled lights of my eyes, we accepted many hardships and faced many experiences so we could establish the state in which we could dedicate ourselves to pray to God, to worship God, to do the five daily prayers to God, to make supplications to Him, to meditate upon Him, to do *dhikr* and *fikr* to Him.

Those who lived before us, our elders, those who lived before our elders, the ancient sages, those who lived before the ancient sages, the *aqtāb*, the *auliyā'*, and the *ambiyā'* have all performed these acts of worship. We know that they also taught us to perform them. We are teaching our relatives, children, and those who will live in a time that is yet to come. Those children will teach those who come after them.

Today we are also engaging in acts of worship that have been taught to us throughout the ages. This is history. The histories have been told. We are doing some of the things that have appeared in those histories.

Now look—*a'ūdhu billāhi minash-shaitānir-rajīm*—there is Mecca. Once a year people go there for hajj. They go to *umrah* as well, all the time, in a state of *maut*, or death, wearing white cloth wrapped around their bodies like a shroud. Thus they proceed in a state of *maut*. That is the determination one must possess—everything in the *dunyā* must be *maut*. They must go on hajj in the same way that the *dunyā* dies for the *mayyit*, the corpse, when it is taken away. They go to find liberation, to fulfill the fifth *fard* of hajj.

In a time that is long gone, the people spoke about those who fulfilled the hajj like that. They said that of the five million, six million, seven million, or ten million people who went to Mecca each year, only one would succeed. The sound of his name would be heard. The name would be called. The other people there then considered such a person a great sage, and they looked for him, discovering who he was and what country he lived in. They visited him to receive good words and good sayings. They went to hear good explanations from that great person. This happened like that for many ages, at the time of Abraham ☮ and before.

They go to fulfill the hajj now in the same way they went then. Long ago they went with death. Now they go without death. Although they wear the same clothes, they do not make their minds and desires die. Their world is not dead, it is alive. They make truth die instead, and they make their desires live. They make the world live and complete the hajj.

Because of this, that sound does not come now. When the people finish hajj, the sound no longer comes—the sound that spoke the name of whoever had successfully completed the hajj. Everything else looks the same, except the sound does not come down.

The *dunyā* and the *ākhirah* became heaven for those who went on hajj and fulfilled the fifth *fard*. Those named by the sound regarded the *dunyā* and the *ākhirah* as heaven. Heaven came into being wherever they were. There was no hell. They reached heaven while they were alive. Heaven was the reward for this hajj.

Someone asked the Rasūl ☻, "Only those who have the means fulfill the hajj. We are the poor. What is going to happen to us? We cannot go there and we cannot return. What should we do? We are poor."

That is why the *dāna-dharmam*, the *sadaqah*, and the fast were decreed: give to the *miskīn*! The people were told to distribute food—those with the means were told that even if they did not fast, they could still obtain the benefit of the fast from distributing food.

Because of this, God said, "Those who do not have the means can complete the hajj every Friday, fifty-two times a year. Those who have the means will go only on one hajj a year."

That refers to the *khutbah*, the Friday sermon in the mosque. Going to the *khutbah* is a hajj. It is *sunnah*, the prayer in which to complete the hajj. God, through the Angel Gabriel ☻, told Rasūlullāh ☻ of this *hājah*, this requirement, for fulfilling the hajj. Thus, the *jum'ah* prayer is like this. It too fullfills the requirement for hajj.

When I was there, wherever there was a mosque, wherever people came for *jum'ah*, there was no salary for the *mu'allim*[1] in those days. They did not pay him. When the people had produce at home or in their gardens, they took a portion of it and gave it to him. The tailor would bring clothing. The matmaker would bring mats. Those who had rice would bring rice. Those who had money brought money. The *mu'allim* would share in their good

---

1. *mu'allim*   the man who teaches the children in the mosque, the caretaker

times and bad, and do his duty. He would officiate for *maut* and *hayāt*, at funerals and weddings. For doing that work he would get one and a quarter rupees for a funeral or a wedding. That was his livelihood for the year. At the time, he was called a *lebbay*. That was how it took place in those days.

It is not like that now. In these times, people do not farm, nor do they do things as they did them in the past. Soon everyone started working at a job and they thought of paying with money. Because of this, the *mu'adhdhin* would spread out a cloth at the Friday *khutbah*. After the prayer, those who were leaving put money into it. They also put money into it when they arrived for prayer. Afterward, the *mu'adhdhin* rolled up the cloth and took it home. That was his income so he could look after his wife and children. That was his income. That was what people did. Now it is not like that either.

Therefore, it is good to give a *hadīyah*, a gift, on Friday. You must endeavor to do this as much as you can. How much you spend when you go on hajj! The Friday prayer is also a hajj. There are two ways you can benefit.

Do this for as long as you possess the *dunyā*.

When the *dunyā* has died away from you, there will no longer be any room for you to give. As long as you possess the *dunyā* and other things, you are a slave to the *dunyā* and those things. As long as you are a slave to them, you do not have God. You need to find a devotee who is a slave to God and obtain liberation through that devotee. This is what we must reflect upon.

Thus, give a *hadīyah* at the Friday prayer. If you can put into the donation box whatever has come into your hands, do that. If there are four Fridays in a month and you go to *jum'ah*, do that.

They will say many things like this in many places. That was one thing that was being said.

However, our family is not like that. We are one family. We, our family, need to act with awareness. If we do not act with awareness, and if instead each person speaks without awareness, saying, "This is the reason! This is the reason! We have to do it like that! We have to do this! We have to take care of this! We have to take care of that! We need to do this! We need to do that!" then we will have to argue for a long time. This is what will happen if each person speaks and acts as he wishes. This is how it is.

My love you. Think about all of this. If you put a donation box in the mosque—we cannot do everything—the children who pray, please put something into it on Fridays. Put a donation into it on a celebration day prayer. Anyone who wishes to do duty to the mosque can put something into it. Yet even if you donate in this way, it will not be enough to do everything that is needed. The accountants can see how much is there and distribute it in a way that is required. This is one way it could be done. Otherwise, each person can donate to a specific section. Let's let that be.

If you can do all this, you will be a family. The mosque is your family. It is your house. It is God's house and your house. It must be managed. The Fellowship is your house too. They are next to each other. One is a place to learn wisdom and the other is God's house, a place to obtain liberation for your soul, a place in which to surrender to Him. They are the pulsebeat of our life. We need both. We—each child—need to work hard for both. We—each child—must be careful to do this.

Whether I will be here or not, cannot be foretold. The children—you—should be here. According to your age, you should be here. When it is time for you to go, your children must endeavor to take care of this place. When it is time for your children to go, their children must endeavor to take care of it. We must teach them like this. When we teach them, we must tell them to go on the good path, the good way, God's path, God's way, with God's qualities. We must train them.

We will have to go.

Teach them truth. Manifest truth. Act as truth and show them. You must try to act according to truth. Very well.

They say there is one hajj a year and that similarly, there is one Lailatul-Qadr a year that comes down on the twenty-seventh day of the fast. The entire world prays *tarāwīh* until just before dawn, praying until *sahar*. They pray and pray, do *dhikr*, and pray and pray. When it is time, they wash their faces and begin to fast. Then they pray *subh, awwal fajr*. This is how they do it.

The world says that the Light comes down on the twenty-seventh day, on Lailatul-Qadr. People have been saying that for a long time.

However, God alone knows the *sirr*, the mystery, of that. The Light comes down continuously. Lailatul-Qadr is Allāh's *rahmah*, His Light. God sends down that Light to the face and the heart of anyone whose intention and whose *qalb* is clear. He fills such people with those beautiful qualities, that Light, and this makes them exalted. He gazes at all who have been filled with His resplendence and who are immersed in it. This brings the *zīnah*, the beauty, to each *qalb*, each heart, each face. This brings the Light to their hearts and makes them resplend. This brings *'ilm*, wisdom, peace, and tranquility to their *qalbs*. If they get it, that is how it will come into being.

We must endeavor to think of this state, jeweled lights of my eyes. If we perceive this state after endeavoring to think of it, this is how it will be.

Even if you are not in the mosque, the children who fast must do it like this. Some of the children leave after praying *maghrib*. Some children leave after praying *'ishā'*. You are fasting and praying, yet you leave after praying *'ishā'*. Some of you leave after *maghrib*. This is not the way to do it. The five daily prayers are *fard* prayers for you and you must endeavor to do them.

It is difficult for you during the days of the fast. Even so, we must experience the difficulty in order to obtain the reward. You must know this. We must experience the difficulty. We cannot only do what is easy for us.

However, even though that is so, they say that today is the twenty-seventh day, called Lailatul-Qadr. They say it is a day that comes once a year, although we cannot say to whom it comes, to whom it goes, and to whom it does not.

It depends upon our own *qalb*. If the *qalb* is clear, we will receive the reward. If our heart and face contain humble qualities, we will receive it. If we surrender to God's will, we will receive it. We will receive it. Thus, this is how it is received once a year on the twenty-seventh day, whether you sleep or you do not sleep.

The twenty-seventh day has arrived. Today is the twenty-seventh. Even if you do not stay throughout the entire night, it would be good if you could stay through *'ishā'* as you usually do—what time does it end—and until the *tarāwīh* prayers are over, instead of running to your homes. We pray *tarāwīh* the easy way, only eight parts out of twenty-one. It is better to pray the entire twenty-one parts, but we have shortened it for your sake. If you could at least stay today, at least for that, it would be good. The children who pray should endeavor to stay through the end of the *tarāwīh* prayer.

If the reward that God gives is there for you, it will be given to you, but you must be ready to accept it. You will get the reward. In doing so, if you do it in the proper way, the correct way, the reward will be there.

Do what you do correctly.
Gather the ingredients you need to make the medicine.

If we do what we do correctly, we will receive the reward. No matter what medicine we make, no matter what illness we make it for, if we gather the correct ingredients and make the medicine correctly, the illness will be cured. It is in this way that we must understand each thing we do.

Thus, children, you must do it like this. It is your responsibility. Even God has said things like this in each age. Endeavor to act accordingly. God alone knows!

You will know the reward. If you are ready, you will get the reward. If the bulb is ready, if the current is ready, the light will come. If neither the bulb nor the current is ready, the light will not come. The light will not come. That is not God's fault. If both the bulb and the current are faulty, the light will not come.

If our faith and our mind are faulty like this, it will not come. If both are correct, the current will flow. You yourselves must see to it and do it. This is what I have to say. This is my part.

You must make every effort to do what needs to be done correctly. Then you can very quickly receive the reward. If you do what you do in a way that is even a little clear, you can very quickly receive it. If you do it in an erratic way, it will be difficult.

However, it is difficult in this country. Now look at certain things. You can come to the mosque to pray *subh* in the morning. It is a little difficult for *zuhr* and *'asr*. You will come to pray for *maghrib*. Somehow you have to pray *zuhr* and *'asr*, according to the *fard*. Your effort must be there. If you want to pray, you can pray wherever you are. All right. This is what I had to tell you.

Today is a good time. Today is the twenty-seventh. If you can do that at this time, it will be good. I have said it. Think about it and then act. I have said it, children, now you can think about it and endeavor to do it. Think about it and do it. If you are exhausted, it is all right. A child who is not tired can do it. However, it is good to stay for *tarāwīh* if you are fasting. It will be better for you. All right. This year we are making it a little shorter. In the future, you decide. *My love you. Āmīn. As-salāmu 'alaikum.* Go eat. Go eat. You have to go to prayers today, so eat. *My love you. My love you. My love you. Anbu. Anbu. As-salāmu 'alaikum.* Go eat. Go eat. *Āmīn.*

Salawāt *for the Prophet Muhammad* ☾.

As-salāmu 'alaikum wa rahmatullāhi. Āmīn. Āmīn. Āmīn. All right. Go eat. Children who are going to pray, pray. Children who are going to eat, eat. If you want to pray, take care of that. Do as much as you can. I said what I had to say. I told you about what existed before. Do as you wish. If you try harder, it will be better. If you try, it will be better.

A'ūdhu billāhi minash-shaitānir-rajīm.
I seek refuge in God from the accursed satan.

Bismillāhir-Rahmānir-Rahīm.
In the name of God, the Most Compassionate, the Most Merciful.

WHEN THE LIGHT DESCENDS
June 14, 1985

O God Most Great, come to us.
O God Most Great, come to us.
O my Treasure of Divine Luminous Bliss!
O Ripe Fruit that fills my *qalb*!
O Creator, O Causal Treasure!
O Precious Jewel, my own radiant gem-studded Lamp!
O King, Master of Ma'shar,
the Assembly at Judgment Day!
He alone is the Light
in the inner realm and the outer realm,
the Ruler of both earthly and heavenly well-being.

You are the only One
for everything in *'ālam* and *'ālamul-arwāh*,
in the world of form and in the world of pure souls.
You alone are the Ruler of my heart.
For my *qalb*, You are the Compassionate One.
You are my Creator.
For my beauty and my *qalb*,
You shine as a beneficent Light.
O wondrous Miracle!
O my wondrous Miracle!
O my God!

May You come to us as Light.
May You come to us as Beauty.

May You come to us as Light.
May You come to us as Beauty.
May You come to us as Wisdom.
May You come to the open space of the heart and
show us the state of truth
as an ever-expanding Resplendence.
You are our Lord—
the Rahmān, the Most Compassionate, Allāh—
who reveals the good qualities.

On that day You were
the Being of Light in the soul.
Now You are the Being of Wisdom
in the house of the soul.
And You are the One who will exist
as the Light in the inner *qalb*.

In the cage that holds life,
You are the Protector who is the Life that protects life.
In our lives You are the One Life that exists as our life.
You are the One who pours out and bestows
the water of the Zam-Zam from the
sea that never runs dry.

You made the Light within the eye and
You made the Beauty of that point of Light
an unparalleled Light, an eye beyond compare.
Into it You placed the subtly luminous earth
that displays so much tranquility
and pours out so much grace.
O miraculous Wonder!
O my God!

It is the same throughout this heart,
throughout this body, in which

there are concealed eyes and unconcealed eyes,
visible eyes and invisible eyes.
Make those eyes clear in Perception and in Awareness.[1]
Make everything clear to Perception, Awareness, and Intellect.
When everything is brought to life
and revealed to those first three levels of wisdom,
transform their state into Assessment.
When that state is understood in Assessment,
make that state subtle.
Transform all those subtle states of wisdom
into the Wisdom that belongs to subtlety.
Transform them into Luminous Wisdom
so that this can be examined and observed.
Transform them into the discerning Light of the Qutb ☉
who knows, deciphers, and sees.

When we understand this state,
transform them all into the qualities of
the seven levels of Wisdom.
Make those levels of wisdom divide the Qur'ān in seven ways.
Transform those seven levels of wisdom into a state
that adds and divides the embryo [from which we took form].
Transform them into the state of the seven levels of Wisdom
that observes and adds and subtracts in my body—
because my body is the Qur'ān—
so we can know it inside and outside, understanding
where to add, where to subtract, and where to join.

There, where this is seen and known and understood,
the well known as Zam-Zam will appear.
The *qalb* will see the state of Ahamad ☉.

---

1. Perception and Awareness   Here Bawangal ☉ is referring to the seven levels of human wisdom: *Unarvu*, Perception; *Unarchi*, Awareness; *Putti*, Intellect; *Madi*, Assessment; *Arivu*, Wisdom; *Pahut Arivu*, Discerning Wisdom; *Pērarivu*, Divine Luminous Wisdom.

The heart and the face will be bright
with the Light of Muhammad ☽.
The eye in your forehead
and in the *'arsh*, the throne of God on the crown of your head,
will open.
To perceive the state of seeing *'ālam* and *'ālamul-arwāh*,
to establish there the praise, *al-hamd*,
to understand all the qualities there,
the fast must be kept with *adab*, with exquisite conduct, as
a fast that restrains each quality,
a fast that restrains each action,
a fast that restrains each evil,
a fast that transforms each state.

Knowing this in every hour and minute,
second after second after second,
understanding and discerning,
seeing and praising only Him
in each second,
we will worship Allāh alone.
He is the One to whom all praise belongs.

O God, we are praising You.
We are praising You and worshipping You.
It is said that
the Light descends while the praise is being given.
After the twenty-seven *hurūf*,
the twenty-seven letters, are seen,
the twenty-eighth luminous letter will be Adam ☽.
The Qur'ān is made of those twenty-seven letters.
When that becomes the place in which the Qur'ān abides,
6,666 *āyāt* will take form in the *sūrah*, the body.

When *Sūratul-Insān*,² is seen,
when that resplendent state is seen,
when the twenty-seven letters become luminous,
when *insān*, the human being, is seen as Adam ☺,
when Adam ☺ assumes the qualities as God,
it is there that the Light will descend on that day.
Allāh will abide in that heart.
The Light will come down to that Qur'ān.
The day the Light descends is the day of wisdom,
the exalted day, the exalted day.
It is then that the body will become a state of Light.
Wisdom and Light will intermingle and abide there.
Allāh will be absolutely everywhere.
This day is the twenty-seventh day of the fast.

Allāhu has shown this to us.
When this is known, that knowledge becomes the fast.
After the open space of the heart is laid open,
after we pray and recite and do our five daily prayers,
when our hearts have dissolved like
earth dissolves in a drenching rain,
then, look, we will understand
the *āyāt* of the Qur'ān.
The power of this decree will be clear within *insān*.
All the meanings will be understood there.
All the explanations and sources
will appear and stand before you.

This is the wonder within *insān*—
the praise, the Rahmān, the blessings,
the recitation of the Qur'ān, the prayers,
the state of love there!

---

2. *Sūratul-Insān*   Bawangal ☺ is layering meanings. *Sūratul-Insān* is Chapter 76 in the Qur'ān. *Sūratul-insān* also means the body of man, the human being.

The *hubb*, all the love we have for Him,
will take the form of the *qudrah*, the power of God.
This will belong only to Allāh.
There is no God other than Him.
All praise and glory are His.
He is the only One that exists—
there is nothing else.

Today is the day we bow down to Him
in the purity of our hearts.
May we place our *qalbs* in His responsibility,
bow our heads before Him,
becoming *ibād*, slaves, worshipping Him.

When we prostrate at His feet,
the grace of the Rahmān
who accepts our prayer
bestows the outcome
of either raising or lowering us.
If He raises us, the day will be Light.

This is the day of liberation,
the day the Qur'ān receives the Light,
the day *insān* becomes worthy,
the day he becomes an *'abd* to God.
Āmīn.

A'ūdhu billāhi minash-shaitānir-rajīm.
I seek refuge in God from the accursed satan.
Bismillāhir-Rahmānir-Rahīm.
In the name of God, the Most Compassionate, the Most Merciful.

It Is All Inside
June 14, 1985

Give the weight of your fast to God and accept from Him what is easy. Keep that in your *qalb*. Fast in this way. Obtain peace. Give the weight to Him. Take the *barakah*. Break your fast. *Al-hamdu lillāh.* All praise belongs to God. *As-salāmu 'alaikum.* May the peace of God be with you. Today is Lailatul-Qadr, the twenty-seventh day of the fast—the prayers may be longer.

Allāh is within you. The power is within you. The rubbish is within you. The goodness is within you. The evil is within you. Everything is within us. We will receive the reward according to the state in which we live. It is all within us. His qualities are within us. His actions are within us. The power is within us. All things—good and evil—are within us. We must understand and know this.

We must cut what needs to be cut and push it aside. If there is a bad part in the food that we cook—whether it is potatoes or anything else—we have to cut it off and push it aside. We have to cut off and push aside the bad part and put the good part in the pot.

No matter how good the food may be, we must cut off and push aside the bad parts that are brought to our minds and take only the good part. No matter how special something may be, we must cut off the bad part and keep only the good part. We should not think, *"This is a delicious thing, it's fine. We can use it all. We can eat it."* If we do that, it will ruin everything. No matter how great a food it is, we must cut off the bad part and use only the good part. Then it will taste good.

Like this, it may appear that there are good things in our lives. But we must cut off the bad parts before we cook them.

Āmīn. Āmīn.

A'ūdhu billāhi minash-shaitānir-rajīm.
I seek refuge in God from the accursed satan.
Bismillāhir-Rahmānir-Rahīm.
In the name of God, the Most Compassionate, the Most Merciful.

Revelation
June 4, 1986

Bawa Muhaiyaddeen ☮ asks Imām Muhammad 'Abdur-Razzaq to recite the Sūratul-Qadr and to say a few words about it. After that, he asks the 'ulamā', the scholars, in the room to speak about Lailatul-Qadr. When they finish speaking, he addresses the man who last spoke.

BAWA MUHAIYADDEEN ☮ What is Qadr?

THE MAN The Night of Decree. It is also called the Night in which Allāh decrees one's destiny; it changes, so it's called power. Also Qadr means decree, to decree.

BAWA MUHAIYADDEEN ☮ Ask the others what is Qadr.

THE SAME MAN The Decree of Destiny!

BAWA MUHAIYADDEEN ☮ *(smiling and referring to the man who just spoke)* He is the one who is always giving the decree. He is continually decreeing.
    Dick Tambi [the *imām*], what do you say?

IMĀM MUHAMMAD 'ABDUR-RAZZAQ All I know is that Bawa has said that it's the night of the ray of Light that comes from Allāh, it's the ray of purity.

BAWA MUHAIYADDEEN ☮ Every year this is the day in the month

of Ramadān in which we worship more, give more *sadaqah*, and fast even more than at hajj time. On this day in Ramadān we do more prayers and perform more acts of worship and *'ibādah*. On this day, man has to think a little for the sake of God. He has to think of this day: Why do we fast? Why do we do all this?

This twenty-seventh day of the fast has been called Lailatul-Qadr by Allāhu ta'ālā in the Qur'ān.

Al-qadā' wal-qadar: the decree and the destiny that is decreed. It is according to Allāh's *qadā'*, His decree, that the *kadir*,[1] the ray of Light, is sent down. *Al-qadā' wal-qadar*. God fully sends down the *rahmah* known as the *mubārakāt*.

He has said:

> I am sending down everything in fullness and giving it to you for the *dunyā* and for the *ākhirah*. May you fully accept it. This is your *qadā'* and *qadar*. Reflect upon it.
>
> I will send down the *qadā'* and the *qadar* in this month according to the duty you have done, as if you were a young child—I will send it down to you according to the *qadā'* and the *qadar*.
>
> Yā Muhammad, this is what I sent down to you on the twenty-seventh day, to you and your *ummah*. Tell them to accept the resplendence, the radiance, the purity, and the fullness of this ray of Light.
>
> The reason for this is that according to your *qadā'*, that which is decreed for you, this is what you yourself have sought, what you yourself have prayed for, what you yourself have intended. This is *qadā'* and *qadar* for you, depending upon the

---

1. *kadir* Bawa Muhaiyaddeen ☮ is layering the meanings of the Arabic word *qadar*, the destiny that is decreed, and the Tamil word *kadir*, ray of Light, to describe how the destiny Allāh sends down to us descends as a resplendent Light.

> state in which you acted. I will send it down according to your intention. This is what you can receive.

That is what Allāh said.

> I will send down My *rahmah*, My Light, according to what you have done. Accept it.

This month, there are prayers that go on throughout the night. This month, the morning prayers in some mosques and some places can last until *zuhr*, the noon prayer, or even until *'asr*, the afternoon prayer.

When those prayers are over they set out the *suhūr*, the meal eaten before dawn prior to beginning the fast. They pray until nearly *sahar*, until just before dawn. Then they have the *suhūr*, then it is *awwal fajr*, then it is time to pray. They finish praying *subh*, and begin to do *dhikr* and say the *salawāt*. They do more prayers, more fully during this month than the other months.

Accordingly, Allāhu ta'ālā Nāyan gives the *rahmah* according to the *qadā'* and the *qadar*.

Sharr and *khair* are in the *tawakkul* of Allāh. *Qadā'* and *qadar*—you will receive the reward according to what you have done. It is certain that Allāh will send down the Light and the *rahmah* upon us. We obtain it according to the reward we seek. We are rewarded for our actions, rewarded for our prayers. He gives to us accordingly on Lailatul-Qadr. This is the way.

How should we seek the reward?

We build a house. Then we need to safeguard it externally by painting it, putting a roof on it, and so forth. We need to care for it. If we care for the house and protect it on the outside, the house will be nice. However nice it looks on the outside, what really matters is inside the house—that the owner, his possessions, his money, his belongings, and decorations are protected. His wealth is inside the house. The inside is what makes the owner comfortable, yet he does have to maintain the outside. He does have to paint it and maintain the roof.

Similarly, we must care for the state of our bodies on the outside. The body has to exist, the body has to be healthy. A human being has to be clean, he has to bathe, he has to eat, and so forth. The body must be cared for. We have to care for our bodies on the outside, stay clean, wear clothing, eat, and so forth. We can do all those things.

However, the real issue is inside.

The Qur'ān is also the same. Although we do have to look after it externally—we have to handle it with respect, study it, and do everything that is required—as to the inner meaning within the Qur'ān, there is a very, very great, great issue. Its outer meaning is engaged in safeguarding *insān*.

However, the Ummul-Qur'ān[2] abides within it.

Everything we study in the Qur'ān is expressed as an outer meaning. All of creation and the things connected to it are described. When you read the Qur'ān from the inside, that part belongs to the *dhāt*, the inner meaning.

This is the inner meaning, that is the outer meaning. Wisdom has to discover the inner meaning—the Ummul-Qur'ān.

God's Words are within it.

Other meanings must come into this through the *wahy*, the revelation. The sound must come; the *salawāt* must come; the speech must come; the warnings must come, warning after warning. That was how it was told to Rasūlullāh ☉. Those sounds must come into the *qalb*. Those sounds must come into wisdom, every word.

When the demons and the devils howl, that is the *dunyā*.

God's sound comes for wisdom, for God's qualities and actions. When the *hasad*, the envy, the robbery, the killing, the sinfulness,

---

2. Ummul-Qur'ān   The Qur'ān is the Mother who is the eye of *'ilm*, wisdom, and *īmān*. It is only when this eye opens that *insān* can understand the Qur'ān.

the karma, and the pride come, that is not God's sound. God's sound is *adhvitam*, non-dualistic. God will say everything He says in a way that is unconditionally right. He will decree everything He decrees in a way that is unconditionally right:

> **This is wrong, reject it! This is right, do it! Tell them, this is not right.**

When that wisdom comes in that state with those words, it is the Ummul-Qur'ān. The Qur'ān is within us—existing within us as an interior place, a secret that we can read. It is very difficult for us to understand what is within. How much more there is inside! For that, we need wisdom. We need God's qualities, His actions, His demeanor, His conduct, His nature.

Everything that must be understood is inside. Even the five daily prayers are inside. If you do not structure your prayer correctly inside yourself, it will not become a prayer on the outside. It will be *bātil*, nullified. You may say you prayed, but it will be *bātil*. It must become *qabūl*, accepted. Each prayer must begin with the intention for it to be accepted. Your *niyyah*, your intention, must exist in an acceptable state. Every context must be acceptable to Allāh. It must be *qabūl*.

For that there must be *hubb*, love. We must be in a state of love, connected to Him. When we say the Kalimah in this state, our *īmān* must be absolutely pure. What should we use to cleanse ourselves? We must wash ourselves with the Kalimah. We must finish cleansing the five sections—earth, fire, water, air, and ether—with the five Kalimāt. Once we have washed, we must know the six articles of faith inside ourselves. We have to open the door and see what is inside.

Similarly, Allāhu ta'ālā Nāyan has created the sky and the earth. We look here and there at the *dunyā*. What have we seen in the *dunyā*? There are so many things. Have we seen them all? No. We have seen a little here, a little there. We have seen only a few, only a few things, in the jungle, in the city. He has placed a museum here, and a zoo. Do they contain everything that exists in the world? No. Only a few things. The world is an enormous museum, a zoo that is like a museum. All kinds of wonders are within it. There are dead things and living things.

As we look at each section, we see that the world is a library. We must read what is inside. As we look at each of the twenty-eight letters, we see that there is a library in each one. We must study what is there and see what wonders are there. Each letter is a library.

Similarly, there are the twenty-seven constellations; the twelve houses of the zodiac; and the *ārudam*, the six-pointed star—the six kinds of wisdom; *panjāngam*, the five elements. People speak of the twelve houses of the zodiac, the twenty-seven constellations.

Allāh has created us with twenty-seven letters, and the twenty-eighth which is *ammāvāsay*, the dark of the moon. The *ārudam* is the six levels of wisdom. The *panjāngam* is the body which is made of the five elements—earth, fire, water, air, and ether. If we look inside ourselves and turn everything upside down, we will see that this body is the *panjāngam*.

The six levels of wisdom are the six kinds of lives—earth-lives, fire-lives, water-lives, air-lives, ether-lives, and the Light-life that is human-life. We must see those lives within the body, where they reside and what they do. There are six kinds of lives—from the first level of wisdom to the sixth that deconstructs and untangles what comes before it. We must see this.

There are twelve houses—the body has twelve openings—two eyes, two ears, two nasal openings, one mouth, the navel, and the two openings below it. That makes ten. The navel has been cut out and sealed. That makes nine openings, nine planets that influence us. The one that was cut out and sealed makes ten. There are two more that are simply there, the *kursī* and the *'arsh*. Those are the twelve openings, twelve houses.

There are twenty-seven constellations, twenty-eight letters. They exist within man—it is his horoscope. We must look at our horoscope. We must look at our state and see which are the auspicious and good planetary influences and which are the inauspicious and evil planetary influences.

Which is good and which is evil? Which is a good statement and which is an evil statement? Which is a good glance and which is an evil glance? Which is a good food and which is a bad food—which one is *halāl* and which one is *harām*? Which is true and which is false?

Thus, there are planets within us that we have to think of, one by one. When we use something evil to accomplish a task, that is an evil, inauspicious influence. When we glance at something with an evil intention, that glance will affect us negatively. When we glance at something with a good intention, it will bring us goodness. Like this, we have to look at all the things within ourselves, study them individually, and understand them.

Everything we seek within is the Qur'ān. That is the Qur'ān. As we cut through each thing, that is *qurbān*, sacrificing the animal qualities within the *qalb*. Do the *qurbān*. Then when you understand and know what is actually there, it will be the Qur'ān for you—that which gives the clear explanation of Allāhu ta'ālā's commandments and states. When you understand everything correctly, it will be the Guru-ān[3] for you. That is the Guru. That is what will exist as the Shaikh. This means: Allāh is the greatest One, the Almighty One. He is not deluded by any of the hypnotic delusions. If your *'ilm* has no delusions, that is *ān*, Qur'ān. If your *'ilm* has entered a delusion and is trapped there, that is not wisdom. It is not *'ilm*, it is a delusion—maya has thoroughly caught you. It must be thrown away.

What we understand without any delusion from the One God is *'ilm*. That wisdom, that *'ilm*, is the *bahrul-'ilm*, the sea of divine knowledge. The Qur'ān is a vast sea. *'Ilm* means we must swim in that sea of divine knowledge with wisdom, with God's qualities. We must swim in that sea, understand, understand,

---

3. Guru-ān   Bawa Muhaiyaddeen ☺ is playing on the words Guru-ān and Qur'ān. Allāh is the Qur'ān that is the Guru and the only Male (*ān*). All the rest of us are female.

and understand what is within it, and do our research. The ocean, the land, the surface of the earth, the underworld, the 'arsh, the kursī, the qalam, heaven, and the eighteen thousand universes are within insān.

There are seven celestial realms, seven colors. There are seven colors in the eye of man and seven colors in the sky. They exist in the body in the same manner. Someone who recites the Qur'ān does so with seven diacritical marks: *fathah, or zabar; kasrah, or zer; dammah, or pēsh; sukūn; nuqtah; tanwīn; shaddah;* and so forth. When we think of how this also exists within us, we see that we must awaken the sounds within us if there is to be any communion between us and God.

If we live according to this state, the ray of Light will come down. Qadā' kadir—the decree is the ray of Light. He will send it down to us as the Rahmatul-'ālamīn and summon us. He will send down the ray of Light. He will send down the Light known as Nūr Muhammad ☙. He will send down that ray of Light.

The *gnāna kan*, the eye of wisdom in the center of the forehead that enables us to understand ourselves and everything else, will be opened. The qalb will sit above the nūn [ن] when the kursī is opened.

When the kursī is opened, he will see both the 'ālam, this physical world, and 'ālamul-arwāh, the world of pure souls. Even if he is here, he can see what is happening there, if he looks. He can see it even if his physical eyes are closed. With that eye he will understand every single thing.

He understands one kind of thing with his qalb through the 'arsh and another through the eye of wisdom, the kursī. He sees one thing through the physical eyes, he sees another through the qalb, and another through the kursī. We can see that state.

The *nafs* and the mind will be like roving, stray dogs. They will always move about aimlessly, without meaning.

Qadā' and qadar come to us according to the state in which we seek the prayers, the worship, the five daily prayers, the good qualities, and actions. God will act according to the *hāl*, the state, of each individual, depending on what that individual is actually doing.

When they say that the *qadar* is sent down in this month, the meaning is that God is sending down to each individual the Light known as the *rahmah*, the ray of Light, the wealth. These are Allāh's words, the words He told the Rasūl ☻ to say. This is the ray of Light God will send down when you meet Him.

We must make our *qalbs* clear like this. When we understand *'ibādah* and what it is to worship Him, Allāhu ta'ālā Nāyan will send down the *rahmah*, the Light, to us.

When Allāh's *wahy*, His revelation, is being sent down, it descends as Light. When it comes to the Angel Gabriel ☻, it arrives as Light. When it emerges from Gabriel ☻, it is *wahy*. When it comes to Rasūlullāh ☻ and is revealed from him, it comes as a commandment and a *hadīth*.

When it comes here, it is transformed into letters. After it comes as letters, it becomes a book. As each *āyah* and each *sūrah*, as each verse and each chapter comes, it becomes a book. When it is read and studied, it becomes a history book. Allāh's commands, the Qur'ān, are then history.

That is how God's words came into the Qur'ān.

If we look further, we see ink and paper. Good and evil, right and wrong appear there—good words as well as bad words. Even *shaitān* is in the Qur'ān. *Shaitān* is a bad word. Allāh is an exalted word. *Harām* means that which has been forbidden. *Halāl* means it is good. That is what it says. We must reject what should be rejected.

It is only when both are there that we can be shown the opposites. Good and evil. When we speak of good and evil, we should see how much evil there is in misconduct, and how much goodness there is in good conduct.

It is not enough just to look at what is good. We must enter into the goodness itself. When we enter a house, there is a room, another room, and another room. This room contains things specific to this room and that room contains things specific to that room. There are so many, so many things—so many events and things in each. You need to see each one.

There are secrets within us just like this. There are so many secrets in the cage of the body. How many secrets there are in the *dunyā*. How many secrets there are in the *ākhirah*. There are secrets in the *awwal*. They are all within us and we must look at and remember and remember each one. When we remember them and understand them, we can know our *rahmah* and greatness.

We need to churn each secret. After we churn milk, what do we see at the end? The curd and the oil. If we heat and clarify the oil, the ghee will come. When we look at ghee, it is like a mirror in which we can see our face and our *sūrah*. If we churn ourselves and see the final result, only Allāh's mirror will be there, just the Light.

When we look at ourselves in the Light, we will have become young, even though we went through so much hardship. What a beautiful form! We will see ourselves. The youthfulness will be visible in us as we proceed and proceed and proceed to reach the *rahmah*—that place will be visible.

Even if you are an old man here, you will be young there. You will be young inside. Even if you have become an old man externally, your youthfulness will be apparent. You are young inside. As we proceed, we will become young.

The celestial beings and the houris will summon you and accompany you. If you do what is right, His ray of Light will come down and summon you. The houris will run next to you and accompany you.

Accordingly, every *niyyah*, every intention, has to come into being in the name of Allāh. Our intentions should be: "You must protect us, O Rahmān! Forgive the mistakes we have made knowingly and unknowingly. How many thoughts come to us every day! How many thoughts come and how we change with each one.

"O God, please stop all of it. Allāh, guide us to the straight path. Even if everything else abandons us, we must never forget You. We must never forget to worship You, pray to You, place our intention upon You, remember You, and think about You with every breath.

"You have to help us. After You help us, You have to open the way and show it to us, Allāh. We must reach peace. You alone are the way to peace and tranquility. There is no one other than You. You alone are the Eternally Able One!

"Accept us. Accept us. This is the only way we can receive the goodness. *Al-hamdu lillāh. Al-hamdu lillāh.*"

There is so much more of this discourse, but it is difficult for me to breathe. I have to stop. Otherwise, I would keep speaking. But I cannot speak with this shortness of breath. It is difficult. *Āmīn. As-salāmu ʿalaikum.* Forgive me.

Salawāt for the Prophet Muhammad ⊕.

Āmīn. As-salāmu ʿalaikum. O God, please help.

All right. It is time now. There is still even a little time left to set out the food for breaking the fast. *Al-hamdu lillāh.*

A'ūdhu billāhi minash-shaitānir-rajīm.
I seek refuge in God from the accursed satan.

Bismillāhir-Rahmānir-Rahīm.
In the name of God, the Most Compassionate, the Most Merciful.

APPENDIX

AL-KALIMĀTUL-K̲H̲AMS
THE FIVE KALIMĀT

Al-Kalimatul-'Ūlā
The First Kalimah

Lā ilāha illAllāh, Muhammadur-Rasūlullāh.
There is no deity other than the One God;
Muhammad is the Messenger of God.

Al-Kalimatut̲h̲-T̲h̲āniyah
The Second Kalimah
Ash-Shahādah
The Affirmation of Faith

*As̲h̲-hadu al-lā ilāha illAllāhu wahdahu lā s̲h̲arīka lah;
wa as̲h̲-hadu anna Muhammadan 'abduhu wa rasūluh.*
I witness that there is no deity other than the One God,
He is One without a partner; and I witness that Muhammad
is His Servant and His Messenger.

Al-Kalimatuth-Thālithah
The Third Kalimah

Subhānallāhi wal-hamdu lillāhi wa lā ilāha illAllāhu wallāhu akbar, wa lā haula wa lā quwwata illā billāhi wa huwal-'alīyul-'azīm.
Glory is God's, and all praise is God's,
and there is no deity other than the One God,
and God is greater,
and there is no majesty and power except with God,
and He is exalted, supreme in glory!

Al-Kalimatur-Rābi'ah
The Fourth Kalimah

*Lā ilāha illAllāhu wahdahu lā sharīka lah;
lahul-mulku wa lahul-hamd; yuhyī wa yumīt;
biyadihil-khair; wa huwa 'alā kulli shay'in qadīr.*
There is no deity other than the One God;
He is One without a partner.
His is the dominion and His is the praise;
He bestows life and death, in His hand is the Good,
and He is omnipotent over all things.

Al-Kalimatul-Khāmisah
The Fifth Kalimah

*Allāhumma inni a'ūdhu bika min an ushrīka bika
shay'aw-wa ana a'lamu bih,
wa astaghfiruka limā lā a'lamu bih,
innaka anta 'ālimul-ghaibi wash-shahādah.
Tubtu 'anhu wa tabarra'tu min kulli dīnin siwā
dīnil-Islām, wa aslamtu laka wa aqūlu:
Lā ilāha illAllāh; Muhammadur-Rasūlullāh.*

Dearest God! I seek protection in You
against ascribing any partner to You knowingly,
and I beg Your forgiveness for that which
I might do unknowingly—
indeed, You are the Knower of both what is seen
and what is hidden. I have turned from such faults
and I absolve myself from every sort of creed except
pure belief in and surrender to You,
and I commit myself wholly to You saying,
"There is no deity other than the One God;
Muhammad is the Messenger of God!"

The Holy Qur'ān Sūratul-'Alaq 96: 1-5

Proclaim! (or Read!) in the name of thy Lord and Cherisher
    Who created—
Created man, out of a (mere) clot of congealed blood:
Proclaim! And thy Lord is Most Bountiful,—
He Who taught (the use of) the pen,—
Taught man that which he knew not.

The Six Articles of Faith

Faith [*al-īmān*] is:
    Belief in Allāh
    Belief in the existence of the angels
    Belief in the books of Allāh which include but are not limited to: the Torah revealed to Moses ⊕, the Psalms revealed to David ⊕, the Gospel revealed to Jesus ⊕, and the Qur'ān revealed to Muhammad ⊕
    Belief in the existence of Allāh's messengers
    Belief in the Last Day, the Day of Resurrection and Judgment
    Belief in the existence of *al-qadr*, Allāh's decree, believing everything that happens ultimately happens by Allāh's decree or permission, whether it appears good or bad to you

A'ūdhu billāhi minash-shaitānir-rajīm.
I seek refuge in God from the accursed satan.
Bismillāhir-Rahmānir-Rahīm.
In the name of God, the Most Compassionate, the Most Merciful.

Glossary

The following traditional supplications in Arabic are used throughout the text:

- ☺ *sallAllāhu 'alaihi wa sallam,* may the blessings and peace of Allāh be upon him, is used following Prophet Muhammad, Rasūlullāh, the Messenger of Allāh ☺.
- ☺ *'alaihis-salām,* peace be upon him, is used following the name of a prophet or an angel.
- ☺ *radiyAllāhu 'anhu* or *'anhā,* may Allāh be pleased with him or her, is used following the name of a companion of the Prophet Muhammad ☺, *aqtāb,* wives of the prophets, and exalted saints.

Unless otherwise noted, the glossary words are Tamil, a Dravidian language whose origins in antiquity are unknown.

Although the glossary has been assembled by editors and translators over the years, a majority of the explanations and definitions have come directly from Bawa Muhaiyaddeen ☺.

Pronunciation Key

The non-Arabic and non-Tamil reader of this book will encounter unknown words and names. We have tried to make them as simple as possible to pronounce.

While there are standard ways of transliterating Arabic letters into Roman script, there is no standard system of transliterating Tamil. Thus, we have not adopted any system in its entirety, but are indebted to many.

We have simplified the consonants—for the typical English speaking person, it would not be particularly helpful to distinguish between the two types of s or h or t in Arabic or the two types of t or the three types of n or l in Tamil.

    dh in Arabic is pronounced like the th in then
    kh in Arabic is pronounced like the ch in Bach
    gn is pronounced like the ñ in the Spanish word *mañana*
    k has been variously transliterated as k or h or g, because its position in the Tamil word determines whether it will be a hard (k) or a soft (h or g) sound
    th (a confusing and inconsistently applied legacy Tamil transliteration that has come down to us from the German) has been simplified throughout as t or d, its hardness (t) or softness (d) depending on its position in the Tamil word. It is never pronounced as an English th.

    Both Arabic and Tamil have long and short vowels: the long vowels have been indicated by long marks in most cases. Thus, in Arabic and Tamil (except where noted):

a	as in agree for Tamil; as in either agree or apple for Arabic, depending on placement
ā	as in father for Tamil; as above with a lengthening of sound for Arabic
i	as in pin
ī	as in pique
u	as in pull
ū	as in rule
o	as in sock
ō	as in ore
e	as in end
ē	as in they

ai   as in aisle, except at the end of a word, where it is generally as in day, for Tamil. In Arabic it may sound either like aisle or day, depending on the letter preceding it.

Any good transliteration system, of course, needs to be logically consistent. However, the idiosyncrasies of both languages must be considered; a few well-placed exceptions serve to clarify a sound that would otherwise be mangled. For instance, *nāi* (dog—pronounced as in high) could not be spelled *nāy* without causing confusion, even though that is what the Tamil spelling would seem to indicate.

A

'abd (Arabic n.) slave, servant

'Abdullāh (Arabic n.) lit. the slave of God

adab (Arabic n.) good conduct, good manners

adhāb (Arabic n.) the punishment

adhvitam (n.) non-duality

ahādīth (sing. *hadīth*) (Arabic n.) the reported words and actions of the Messenger of God ☮

Ahamad ☮ (Tamil & Arabic n.); *ahmad* ☮ (Arabic n.) The beauty of the heart that brings beauty to the countenance (*muham,* Tamil n.) is Muhammad ☮, the Messenger of God. That beauty is the beauty of Allāh's qualities. This is a name that comes from within the ocean of divine knowledge, *bahrul-'ilm*. Allāh is the One who is worthy of the praise of the heart. Lit. most praiseworthy

ākhirah (Arabic n.) The kingdom of God; *ākhirah* is where the soul proclaims the First Kalimah to Allāh. "There is nothing but You, O Allāh!" This is the ultimate and final realization, the soul's exclamation as it perceives who it is, and with this final realization and expression, the soul that is a ray of God's Light returns to the One Omnipresent God. The soul returns to the Source from which it came. There is only One— Allāh. Where all this happens is called *ākhirah*.

ākhiratuz-zamān (Arabic phrase) the time of the *ākhirah*

'ālamul-arwāh (Arabic phrase) the world of pure souls

al-hamdu (Arabic n.) the praise

al-hamdu lillāh (Arabic phrase) all praise is to Allāh

alif (Arabic n.) Arabic letter corresponding to the English letter "a"

Allāh, Allāhu (Arabic n.) God, who is One and in Oneness with all lives

Allāhu *akbar* (Arabic phrase) God is greater

Allāhu ta'ālā (Arabic phrase) God, the exalted

Allāhu ta'ālā Nāyan (Arabic and Tamil phrase) God, the exalted Lord

ambiyā' (sing. *nabī*) (Arabic n.) prophets

āmīn (Arabic n.) may it be so

ān (n.) male

ammāvāsay (n.) the dark of the moon, the new moon

anbu (n.) love

aqtāb (sing. Qutb☺) (Arabic n.) those exalted being(s) sent by Allāh through His grace and mercy, to reawaken humankind's faith in God and to establish certitude in our hearts

arivu (n.) wisdom, the fifth level of human wisdom

'arsh (Arabic n.) The throne of God; the plenitude from which God rules; the place on the crown of the head is the throne that can bear the weight of Allāh. Allāh is so heavy that we cannot carry the load with our hands or legs. The *'arsh* is the only part of the human being that can support Allāh.

ārudam (n.) astrology

al-asmā'ul-husnā (Arabic phrase) The plenitude of the ninety-nine duties of God; the manifestations of His essence of grace, the *sifāt* of His *dhāt*. His qualities are the manifestations which emerge from Him. When God performs His duty, these manifestations of His essence are brought into action; His qualities become His *wilāyāt* or duties. Lit. the beautiful names

'asr (Arabic n.) The afternoon prayer; *'Asr* is the heart, a soft pouch of water where air and water intermingle. Because air and water are within us in the lungs and in the heart, they are connected

to us. Earth, water, and air are connected. We must know this as we cut away these connections and establish a connection with the Light of God.

as-salāmu 'alaikum (Arabic phrase) The peace of God be upon you.

as-salāmu 'alaikum wa rahmatullāhi (wa barakātahu kulluhu) (Arabic phrase) The peace and compassionate grace (and blessings) of God be upon you.

A'ūdhu billāhi minash-shaitānir-rajīm (Arabic phrase) I seek refuge in God from the accursed satan

auliyā' (Arabic n.) saints; guides; friends of Allāh

awwal fajr (Arabic n.) the early morning prayer performed before the *subh* prayer

āyāt (sing. *āyah*) (Arabic n.) verses in the Qur'ān; signs or miracles

B

bādushāh (Arabic n.) king

bahrul-'ilm (Arabic phrase) the ocean of divine knowledge

barakah (Arabic n.) blessing

bātil (Arabic n.) nullified, invalid

Bismillāhir-Rahmānir-Rahīm (Arabic phrase) In the name of God, the Most Compassionate, the Most Merciful.

bismin-kai (Arabic and Tamil phrase) the node of flesh on the physical heart where our good and evil deeds are recorded, much like the black box on aircraft

D

dammah; pesh (Arabic; Urdu n.) the vowel point for "u"

dāna-darumam (n.) distributing food to the poor

daulat (Urdu n. borrowed from the Arabic n. *dūlah*) Wealth, the wealth of the grace of God. The wealth of Allāh is the wealth of divine knowledge; the wealth of perfect *īmān*.

dhāt (Arabic n.) the essence of the grace of God

dhikr (Arabic n.) The remembrance of God; of the many *dhikrs*, the most exalted *dhikr* is, "*Lā ilāha illAllāhu*: There is nothing other than You, (O God.) Only You are Allāh." All *dhikrs* relate to His *wilāyāt* or His actions, but this *dhikr* points to Him and to Him alone.

dīn (Arabic n.) the path of absolute purity; a formal spiritual path or religion

Dīnul-Islām (Arabic phrase) The path of absolute purity that is Islām. He who is in Dīnul-Islām gives peace to all living beings, he makes them tranquil, he gives them love and he embraces them. He embraces them to his bosom and to his heart with unity and love, as one form to another. He greets others face to face, embraces them, showing love to love. He who embraces another in this manner is in Dīnul-Islām.

dunyā (Arabic n.) the world

F

fard (pl. *furūd*) (Arabic n.) obligatory religious duty(ies)
fathah; zabar (Arabic; Urdu n.) the vowel point for "a"
fikr (Arabic n.) constant contemplation and immersion in Allāh
firdaus (Persian n.) paradise

G

gnāna kan (n.) the eye of wisdom on the center of the forehead
gnānam (n.) knowledge, wisdom, divine wisdom, wisdom awakened by grace; knowledge of the divine
gnāni (n.) a person of wisdom
Guru (n.) Teacher; Allāh is the Guru.
Guru-ān (Tamil phrase) The Guru (Allāh) is the only Male, all the rest of us are female. This meaning is layered with the Arabic word Qur'ān: that which gives the clear explanation of Allāhu ta'ālā's commandments and states. When you understand everything correctly, it will be the Guru-ān for you. That is the Guru. That is what will exist as the Shaikh. This means: Allāh is the greatest One, the Almighty One. He is not deluded by any of the hypnotic delusions. If your 'ilm has no delusions, that is ān, Qur'ān. If your 'ilm has entered a delusion and is trapped there, that is not wisdom. It is not 'ilm, it is a delusion—maya has thoroughly caught you. It must be thrown away.

H

hadīth (pl. *ahādīth*) (Arabic n.) the reported words and actions of the Messenger of God ☮

hadīyah (Arabic n.) gift

hājah (Arabic n.) requirement

hajj (Arabic n.) holy pilgrimage

hāl (Arabic n.) state

halāl (Arabic n.) acceptable to God; permissible; that which conforms to the commands of God

harām (Arabic n.) forbidden by God; impermissible; that which does not conform to the commands of God

hasad (Arabic n.) envy

hayāh (Arabic n.) life; lifetime

hayawān (Arabic n.) animal

hubb (Arabic n.) love

hurūf (Arabic. n.) letters

I

'*ibād* (sing. '*abd*) (Arabic n.) slaves, servants

'*ibādah* (Arabic n.) service to God performed with a melting heart

illAllāh(u) (Arabic n.) Only You are God. You alone exist.

'*ilm* (Arabic n.) knowledge of the divine

imām (Arabic n.) the leader of the prayers at the mosque

īmān (Arabic n.) absolute and unshakable faith that God alone exists; the complete acceptance by the heart that God is One

Īmān-Islām (Arabic n.) Perfect certitude and purity of faith in Allāh; the state of the spotlessly pure heart which contains Allāh's Holy Qur'ān, His divine radiance, His divine wisdom, His truth, His prophets, His angels, and His laws. When the resplendence of Allāh is seen as the completion within this pure heart of man, that is Īmān-Islām. When the complete, unshakable faith of this pure heart is directed towards the One who is Completeness and is made to merge with that One; when that heart trusts only in Him and worships only Him, accepting Him as the only perfection and the only One worthy of worship—that is Īmān-Islām.

al-injīl (Arabic n.) Christianity

insān (Arabic n.) man, a human being

Insān Kāmil (Arabic n.) a perfected human being; one who has realized Allāh as his only wealth, cutting away the wealth of the world and the wealth sought by the mind; one who has acquired God's qualities, performs his own actions accordingly, and immerses himself within those qualities; one in whom everything other than Allāh has been extinguished

iqra' bismi rabbikal-ladhī khalaq (Arabic phrase) Proclaim! (or Read) in the name of thy Lord and Cherisher Who created— (*Sūratul-'Alaq*, 96:1). This was the first verse of the Qur'ān to be revealed.

'ishā' (Arabic n.) The evening prayer which is offered after darkness has fallen. We must understand how the body is made to die, how the soul is transformed into Light, how the loan is repaid— we must give the loan of the body back to God's responsibility. That is the day we will see Allāhu as the only One that remains.

Islām (Arabic n.) purity; unity; the state of total and unconditional surrender to the will of God; the state of absolute purity; to accept the commands of God and His qualities and actions and to establish that state of purity within oneself, worshipping Him alone

J

al-jabbūrat (Arabic n.) the scripture of Zoroastrianism; Fire-Worship

jahannam (Arabic n.) the lowest hell

jinn (Arabic n.) a being created of fire

jum'ah prayer (Arabic n.) the midday prayer in the mosque performed on Fridays after the sermon

K

kadir, kadir oli (n.) ray, ray of light

kāfir (Arabic n.) a person from whom the truth is hidden; an unbeliever

Kalimah (pl. Kalimāt) (Arabic n.) *Lā ilāha illAllāhu:* There is nothing other than You, O God. Only You are Allāh. Lit. There is no deity other than You, O God. Only You are God. The recitation or remembrance of God that cuts away the influence of the five elements of earth, fire, water, air, and ether, washes away all the karma that has accumulated from the very beginning until now, dispels the darkness, beautifies the heart and causes it to become resplendent. The Kalimah washes the body and the heart of man and makes them pure, makes man's wisdom emerge and impels that wisdom to know the self and God.

kāmil (Arabic n.) perfection

al-Karīm (Arabic n.) God, the Most Generous

kasrah, zer (Arabic; Urdu n.) the vowel point for "i"

khair (Arabic n.) that which is right or good; that which is acceptable to wisdom and to Allāh, as opposed to *sharr,* that which is evil or bad

khidmah (Arabic n.) duty, service

khutbah (Arabic n.) a sermon given at the Friday prayer, *'īd* prayers, and other occasions such as the eclipse prayer and weddings

kursī (Arabic n.) Allāh's seat in the forehead between the eyes; the eye of wisdom between the physical eyes in the center of the forehead

L

lā ilāha illAllāhu (Arabic phrase) There is nothing other than You, (O God). Only You are God. This is explained by Bawa Muhaiyaddeen ☉ in the ultimate sense of Sufism as *lā maujūda illAllāh* (there is nothing that exists except God).

Lailatul-Qadr (Arabic phrase) The Night of Power (or Destiny or Decree)

lām (Arabic n.) Arabic letter corresponding to the English letter "l"

lebbay (n.) *mu'adhdhin* (Arabic n.) the caretaker of the mosque who recites the call to prayer

M

maddah (Arabic n.) a diacritic that indicates an extra long vowel

maghrib (Arabic n.) the prayer performed just after sunset

mahr (Arabic n.) mandatory payment, bridal gift or dowry

malā'ikah (Arabic n.) angels, archangels

ma'shar (Arabic n.) the assembly that gathers at Judgment Day

maut (Arabic n.) death

maya (n.) The glitters seen in the darkness of illusion; the 105 million glitters seen in the darkness of the mind which result in 105 million rebirths. Maya is a *shakti*, an energy, that can take many, many millions of hypnotic forms. If man tries to grasp these forms with his intellect, though he sees the form, he will never be able to catch it, for it will elude him by taking another form. Maya is a *shakti* which takes on various shapes, causes man to forfeit his wisdom, and confuses and hypnotizes him into a state of torpor. This word has many meanings. Lit. illusion

mayyit (Arabic n.) corpse

mīm (Arabic n.) Arabic letter corresponding to the English letter "m"

mi'rāj (Arabic n.) Prophet Muhammad's ☻ miraculous night journey to Jerusalem, then up through the seven heavens, to the Throne of God and back

miskīn (Arabic n.) a poor person

mu'adhdhin (Arabic n.) the man who recites the call to prayer; the caretaker of the mosque

mu'allim (Arabic n.) the man who teaches the children at the mosque, the caretaker

mubārakāt (Tamil & Arabic n.) The blessings of God's love in all three worlds, the *awwal*, the *dunyā*, and the *ākhirah*. Allāh's wealth is the wealth of the soul, of wisdom, and of His grace, which is the resplendent wisdom of the Nūr. *Mu* (n.) is a Tamil prefix meaning three; *barakāt* (Arabic n.) means blessings.

muham (n.) face, countenance

Muhammad ☻ (Arabic n.) The beauty of the Light of Allāh's essence present in the heart and reflected in the face is the

Messenger of God ☻. Muhammad, the Messenger of God ☻, is the last of the line of prophets.

Muhammadur-Rasūlullāh ☻ (Arabic phrase) Muhammad ☻, the Messenger of Allāh

mu'min (pl. *mu'minūn*) (Arabic n.) believer(s)

musallā (Arabic n.) prayer mat

Muslim (Arabic n.) A person who has declared his faith in God. He who accepts God accepts the truth. Anyone who understands this truth and who obtains Allāh's qualities, who acts with Allāh's actions, who makes peace, who regards the lives of others as his own life, and who acts with Allāh's qualities is a person of purity. Such a person is a Muslim—Islām means purity. He who helps another who is suffering, he who helps another who is in pain, he who helps another who is hungry is a Muslim. He can be called a Muslim. He who brings another person to his own state of peace is a Muslim. He who experiences the pain of another as his own pain is a Muslim. Allāh will bless anyone who thinks these kinds of good thoughts.

N

nabī (pl. *ambiyā'*) (Arabic n.) prophet(s)

nafs (Arabic n.) the self from which the desires arise; lit. person, spirit, personality, inclination, or desire which goads or incites one towards evil

nafs ammārah (Arabic n.) the seven desires which goad and incite one towards evil

najjām (Arabic n.) ancient astronomers

nasīb (Arabic n.) fate, destiny

Nāyan (n.) Lord; a term of respect added in Tamil to Allāhu ta'ālā

ni'mah (Arabic n.) a gift of grace; beneficial blessing; boon

niyyah (Arabic n.) intention

nūn (Arabic n.) Arabic letter corresponding to the English letter "n"

nuqtah (Arabic n.) the dots placed over or under Arabic letters to differentiate between them

Nūr (Arabic n.) Light; the resplendence of Allāh; the plenitude of the Light of Allāh that has the resplendence of a hundred million suns; the completeness of Allāh's qualities. When the plenitude of all these becomes One and becomes resplendent as One, that is His Light, His Nūr. That is Allāh.

Nūr Muhammad ☥ (Arabic phrase) the Light, the Completion that is Muhammad ☥

P

Pahut Arivu (phrase) Discerning Wisdom, the sixth level of human wisdom

panjangam (n.) the five bodies, the five elements

Pērarivu (n.) Divine Luminous Wisdom, the seventh level of human wisdom

putti (n.) intellect, the third level of wisdom

Q

qabr (Arabic n.) the grave

qabūl (Arabic n.) accepted

qadā' (Arabic n.) the decree

qadā' kadir (Tamil and Arabic n.) A layered meaning: Someone who recites the Qur'ān does so with seven diacritical marks—*fathah, zabar; kasrah, zer; dammah, pēsh; maddah; sukūn; nuqtah; tanwīn; shaddah;* and so forth. When we think of how this also exists within us, we see that we must awaken the sounds within us if there is to be any communion between us and God. If we live according to this state, the ray of Light will come down. *Qadā' kadir*—the decree is for the ray of Light. He will send it down to us as the Rahmatul-'ālamīn and summon us. He will send down the ray of Light. He will send down the Light known as Nūr Muhammad ☥.

al-qadā' wal-qadar (Arabic phrase) the decree and the destiny that is decreed

qadr (Arabic n.) power, destiny, decree

qalam (Arabic n.) the mighty Pen that writes Allāh's will

qalb (Arabic n.) The heart, the heart within the heart of man, the innermost heart. Bawa Muhaiyaddeen ☥ explains that there are two states for the *qalb*. The first state is made up of four chambers, which are Hinduism, Fire-Worship, Christianity, and Islām. The second state is the flower of grace, the *rahmah*. Inside these four chambers there is a flower, the flower of the *qalb* that is the divine qualities of Allāh. God's fragrance exists within this inner *qalb*.

Qiyāmah (Arabic n.) the Day of Resurrection

al-Quddūs (Arabic n.) the Holy One

qudrah (Arabic n.) the power of God

Qur'ān (Arabic n.) The words of Allāh that were revealed to His Messenger, Prophet Muhammad ☺. Those words that came from Allāh's power are called the Qur'ān; Allāh's inner book of the heart; the Light of Allāh's grace that comes as a resonance from Allāh.

Qur'ān Sharīf (Arabic phrase) The Noble Qur'ān

qurbān (Arabic n.) Inwardly, it is to purify one's innermost heart, by sacrificing and cutting away the animal qualities that exist within the self, thus making one's life *halāl,* acceptable to God. The SubhānAllāhi Kalimah is recited for the purpose of destroying these animal qualities within the *qalb.* Outwardly, it is the ritual sacrifice of animals to make them *halāl.*

Qutb ☺ (pl. *aqtāb*) (Arabic n.) One who is endowed with the power of the light of grace-awakened Discerning Wisdom that dawned from the throne of God and that investigates, understands, and examines everything in the eighteen thousand universes and beyond. Through this inner analysis, the darkness of evil is dispelled and the beauty of goodness is made clear and radiant. The Qutb ☺ is sent by Allāh, through His grace and mercy, to reawaken mankind's faith in God and to establish certitude in our hearts. He is the wondrous embodiment and illustration of *īmān,* absolute faith in God, in all three worlds.

Qutbiyyah (Arabic n.) the state of the Qutb ☺; Pahut Arivu, the sixth level of wisdom, the state that explains the truth of God to the human soul

R

Rabb (Arabic n.) God, the Lord, the Creator and Cherisher of all lives

Rabbal-'ālamīn (Arabic phrase) the Lord of all the worlds
Raḥīm (Arabic n.) God, the Most Merciful
raḥmah (Arabic n.) compassion, grace, mercy
Raḥmān (Arabic n.) God, the Most Compassionate
Raḥmatul-'ālamīn (Arabic phrase) the Mercy for All the Universes, the One who gives everything to all His creations
Ramadān (Arabic n.) the month of fasting
Rasūl, Rasūlullāh (Arabic n.) messenger, Messenger of Allāh, most often referring to Prophet Muhammad ☮.
rizq (Arabic n.) nourishment provided by Allāh, sustenance
rūh (Arabic n.) The soul, the Ray of Light belonging to God; the Light of God's wisdom. Bawa Muhaiyaddeen ☮ explains that the *rūh* is life, *hayāh*. Out of the six kinds of lives, the soul is the Light life, the human life. It is a ray of the Nūr, the Light of Allāh, a ray that does not die or disappear. It comes from Allāh and returns to Allāh.
rukū' (Arabic n.) the bowing position in prayer
rusul (sing. *rasūl*) (Arabic n.) messengers

S

sabab (Arabic n.) means
sabūr (Arabic n.) Patience; inner patience; to go within patience, to accept it, to think and reflect within it. *Sabūr* is that patience deep within patience which comforts, soothes, and alleviates the suffering caused by the mind. Lit. *sabūr* is the intensive form of *sabr*
sadaqah (Arabic n.) charity
sahar (Arabic n.) the time immediately before dawn, before the call to prayer
salām (Arabic n.) peace; also refers to the greeting of peace: "Peace be upon you."
salāmah (Arabic n.) safety and security
salawāt (Arabic n.) the recitation of peace and blessings upon the Rasūl ☮; prayers or blessings; usually used to refer to the supplications asking God to bless the prophets and mankind

shaddah (Arabic n.) a diacritic indicating doubling of letters
Shaikh (Arabic n.) Teacher
shaitān (Arabic n.) satan
sharr (Arabic n.) that which is bad or evil
shart (Arabic n.) condition, rule
shukūr (Arabic n.) intense gratitude; contentment with whatever may happen, realizing that everything comes from Allāh; contentment arising from gratitude
sifāt (Arabic n.) The physical world of form, creation, manifestation. Lit. Something that describes. Thus the ninety-nine names of Allāh are known as *sifātullāh*.
sindanay (n.) the remembrance of how we once existed with God in the world of pure souls
sirr (Arabic n.) Mystery, secret, divine mystery; traditionally in Sufism this refers to the innermost (secret) heart or *qalb*.
subh (Arabic. n.) the early morning prayer; the prayer in which the connection to the earth is cut
Sufi(s) (Arabic n.) A Sufi exists in the absolute silence of Light within God. He prays with God as God. He performs 43,242 prostrations to God each day. His every breath, every intention, every thought goes out to unite with God. His heart is open and melting with love. He does not harm anyone or kill anything. He feels the suffering of others as his own. He does not belong to any one race or religion. He lives in a state of unity with all lives. He does not dance or take intoxicants. His sustenance is God.
suhūr (Arabic n.) the meal eaten before dawn prior to beginning the fast
sukūn (Arabic n.) the small circle used to mark the absence of a vowel
sunnah (Arabic n.)
sūrah (Arabic n.) chapter (beginning with the letter س)
sūrah (Arabic n.) form, body (beginning with the letter ص)
Sūratul-Insān (Arabic phrase) This has a double meaning: Chapter 76 of the Qur'ān; the form of man.

Sūratul-Qadr (Arabic phrase) This has a double meaning: Chapter 97 of the Qurʾān; the form of the power of the ray of Light that comes from God.

T

tambi (n.) younger brother

tanwīn (Arabic n.) nunation, where "in," "an," or "un" are added as suffixes to show the case

tarāwīh (Arabic n.) the prayers performed during Ramadān after ʿishāʾ

tasbīh (Arabic n.) recitations that glorify Allāh; a *dhikr* glorifying God in a state of true prayer

taubah (Arabic n.) repentance

tauhīd (Arabic n.) the affirmation of the unity of Allāh; the state of oneness without any trace of duality; the indivisible and absolute Oneness of God

tawakkul (Arabic n.) trust (in Allāh)

Tiru Maray (Tamil phrase) the Divine, Hidden Treasure, al-Furqān; the Divine Qurʾān; the Divine Book

tiyānam (n.) meditation

toluhay (n.) prayer, specifically the five-times prayer

U

ummah (Arabic n.) followers, people, community, nation, family

Ummī (Arabic n.) unlettered, mute; refers to the Messenger of God ☻

Ummul-Qurʾan (Arabic phrase) The Qurʾān is the mother who is the eye of *ʿilm*, wisdom, and *īmān*. It is only when this eye opens that *insān* can understand the Qurʾān.

unarchi (n.) sense awareness, the second level of wisdom

unarvu (n.) sense perception, the first level of wisdom

V

vanakkam (n.) prayer, worship

W

wahy (Arabic n.) revelation
waqt (Arabic n.) a point in time
wilāyāt (Arabic n.) the miraculous duties and actions of Allāh
wuḍū' (Arabic n.) ablution

Y

yā (Arabic inter.) O; an exclamation of praise, an interjection of greatness or praise
yā Allāh (Arabic phrase) O Allāh

Z

az-Zabūr, al-Jabbūrat, al-Injīl, and al-Furqān (Arabic n.) the scriptures of Hinduism, Fire-Worship, Christianity, and Islām; Hinduism, Fire-Worship, Christianity, and Islām
Zam-Zam (Arabic n.) The outer Zam-Zam is a well located within the Masjid al-Harām in Mecca. It is a miraculously generated source of water from God. Thousands of years ago when Abraham's☺ infant son, Ishmael☺, was left with his mother Hagar☺ in the desert, God sent Angel Gabriel☺, who kicked the barren ground, and the water rose.
zīnah (Arabic n.) beauty
zuhr (Arabic n.) the noon prayer; the prayer that cuts the connection to elemental air and takes in the air of the Light of the soul to God's section

Index

Passim denotes that the references are not to be found on all of the listed pages; e.g., 24-29 *passim* would be used where the reference is on pages 24, 25, 27, and 29.

'*abd* (slave) to Allāh. *See* Allāh, '*abd* to
Adam ☺, 89
  created by Allāh, 28, 43
  and Eve ☺, 26, 43
age, when wisdom comes man has no, 70
Ahamad ☺, when the *qalb* becomes, 49
air, cut the connection to, 72
ākhirah (God's kingdom), 29, 70
Allāh (God)
  '*abd* to, 13-14, 19-20, 44
  grace of, 23
  is within us, 91
  Light of, 5-6, 15-22 *passim*, 69-71, 74, 82, 85-90
  the One, 8-10, 14, 23, 31-33, 38, 46
  rahmah of, 23, 28, 34-37 *passim*, 51-57 *passim*, 60-61
    women are sent by the, 43-44
  sound of—comes, 2-5 *passim*
  the Supreme Being, 37-38
  See also God
al-qadā' wal-qadar (the Decree and what is decreed), 94

ambiyā' (prophets), God sent the, 63-65
ammāvāsay (new moon), 26, 49, 69-70
Angel Gabriel ☺. *See* Gabriel ☺, Angel
aqtāb (pl. of Qutb ☺), 34, 37, 63-64. *See* Qutb ☺
astronomers, ancient, 63
auliyā' (saints, guides) came, 63-65

baby, become a—to Allāh, 25-26, 32-33
bahrul-'ilm (ocean of divine knowledge), 4
bātil (invalid), 97
begging, no—in Islām, 57-58
bismin-kai (a small node of flesh on the heart), 16
body(ies)
  all—contain the five elements, 37
  bring light to the, 86-89
  care for the, 96
  do *wudū'* in the *qalb* to prevent a sick, 40
  is salty, 3-4

127

body(ies) *(continued)*
  is the Qur'ān, 87
  sick, 40
  twelve openings of the, 98
book, Allāh's commands are a history, 101
breath(s)
  correct the, 39
  two, 72
bulb, if the—is ready, the Light will come, 83

charity, give, 46, 67
child(ren)
  do *tasbīh* as a—in the womb, 24-27 *passim*
  teach your, 81
colors, seven, 100
constellation(s)
  each letter is a, 26-27, 34
  twenty-seven, 98
crescent moon, 70
current, if the—is ready, the Light will come, 83-84

dāna-darumam (charity), 67
darkness, when wisdom comes there is no, 70
day
  of darkness, 26, 49
  twenty-seventh, 27, 48-49, 74, 82-84, 94
  See also Lailatul-Qadr
death
  die before, 70-73
  state of, 47-48
destruction
  of the *dunyā* held back by the Light, 51
  path of, 10

diacritical marks awaken the sounds within, 100
diseases, cut away all, 41-42, 47-48
doctor for the soul, 36
donation box in mosque, 81
dunyā (world), 97
  destruction of the—is held back, 51
  imperfect, 10
  is dark, 70
  making the—die, 72, 80
duties, five obligatory, 15, 48, 53-54, 68

elements
  cut the connections to the, 72
  five, 31, 37, 98
embryo, man becomes an—within God, 32-33
enemy of Islām is evil qualities, 59
evil
  and good, 99, 101
  qualities, 59, 61

family, our—must act with awareness, 80-81
fast(ing)
  benefits of, 79
  give the weight of your—to God, 91
  God decrees the, 10-15 *passim*, 20
  with exquisite conduct, 88
  inner meaning of, 60
  of Ramadān, 24, 51-57
  realize this, 47
  reasons for the, 54
  why we, 67-68

fire of hunger, 52–56
food
  cut off the bad part of, 91
  distribute, 79
fruit on trees is for everyone, 53
furūd. See duties, five obligatory

Gabriel ☮, Angel, 16, 101
  reveals the Qur'ān, 1–5 *passim*
gnānis (wise men) can see in the dark, 70
God
  as a servant, 43
  bestows His wealth, 63–65, 71
  comes to us, 85–86
  created man, 31–33
  Day of, 39
  decree of, 93–94
  decrees the fast, 10–20 *passim*
  duty of, 64
  house of, 81
  insān belongs to, 53
  intend, 102–103
  is ready, 64–66, 73, 75
  kingdom of, 77
  Light of. *See* Allāh, Light of
  man
    becomes an *'abd* to, 44
    becomes an embryo within, 32–33
  the One, 31
  praising, 88–90
  pray to, 77
  property of, 44–46
  protects our wealth, 36
  rahmah of, 11–21 *passim*, 43–44
  representatives of, 34–35
  revealed *īmān*, 11–14, 18–21
  reward of, 71–74 *passim*, 83–84
  sent the prophets, 66

God *(continued)*
  sound of, 96–97
  speech existing within, 73
  takes nine steps towards man, 45
  treasures of, 65, 72–73
  wealth of, 63–65, 71, 75
  worship—within your *qalb*, 27–29, 42–46 *passim*
  See also Allāh
good and evil, 99, 101
grace, three thousand kinds of, 69

hadīyah (gift), 58, 80
hajj (holy pilgrimage)
  complete the, 47-48
  go on, 68, 78–81 *passim*
health and hygiene, 40–42, 48–49
heaven was the reward of hajj, 79
horoscope, 98
house
  inside the, 95–96
  your—and God's, 81
hunger, see your own—and that of others, 47, 50-57, 66–68

'ibādah (service or prayer to God), 73
illnesses, look for a doctor to cure our, 35-36
'ilm (divine knowledge), 99
  path of, 12–21 *passim*
  study, 35–37, 45
īmān (faith, certitude and determination)
  God revealed, 11–14, 18–21
  strengthen your, 45–46
insān (man), 89–90
  belongs to God, 53

insān (man) *(continued)*
   everything is given to, 8–9
   is formed of twenty-eight letters, 26–27, 31-34 *passim,* 49
   kāmil, 5–6, 12–14, 20, 29
inside, everything that needs to be understood is, 97
intention(s)
   make your, 73
   in the name of God, 102
Islām
   evil qualities are the enemy of, 59
   meaning of, 57–60

Judgment Day, 38–39
jum'ah (Friday prayer), go to, 79–81

kadir (ray of light), 5
Kalimah, (remembrance of God), 52-53, 97
khidmah (duty) done by a woman, 43
khutbah (Friday sermon) is a hajj, 79
kursī (eye of wisdom), 28, 100

Lailatul-Qadr (Night of Power), 15–22 *passim,* 23–31 *passim* 48-49, 51–52, 55–60 *passim,* 69, 71, 74, 82
   comes once a year, 5–6
   See also day, twenty-seventh
letters
   twenty-eight, 26, 28, 31, 49
   twenty-seven, 26–27, 34, 48–49, 82-83, 88–89
library, each letter is a, 98

Light
   of Allāh. *See* Allāh, Light of
   comes when bulb and current are ready, 83
   of Nūr Muhammad ☮, 48–49
   ray(s) of, 24-26, 51–60 *passim,* 69–71, 74, 93–95, 100–102

man
   all is within, 37, 91
   becomes an *'abd* to God, 13-14, 19-20, 44
   formed of twenty-eight letters, 26
   God created, 31–33
   has become rich, 67
   must be ready, 64–66, 73
   must understand himself, 29–35 *passim,* 49
   today is—'s day, 39
maut (death), 78
medicine, make the—correctly, 83
mīm (Arabic letter), 48
mind, fire in man's, 55–56
mistakes, repent for your, 38–39
Monday we are born, 68
mosque, donation box in, 81
mu'adhdhin (caretaker of mosque), 80
mubārakāt (blessings of God), 77
Muhammad ☮, *ummah* of, 11–14 *passim,* 18-20, 38–40, 44–48 *passim*
   See also Rasūl ☮
mu'min (believer), become a, 13, 18–20, 29–31, 34, 60
museum, the world is a, 97–98

Muslim, meaning of, 59–60

night, dark, 70
Night of Power. *See* Lailatul-Qadr
Nūr Muhammad ☺, Light of, 17–20 *passim*, 27–28, 48–49
Nūr (Light) within the Nūr, 13–14

ocean water turns sweet, 1–2
one, only
  correctly completes the fast, 69
  successfully completes the hajj, 55, 60, 69
oneself, know. *See* man must understand himself

path
  of destruction, 10
  of 'ilm, 12–21 *passim*
peace, obtain, 77
planets within, 99
prayer(s)
  completed, 70
  five times of, 42, 44, 71–72, 82, 84
  leaving—early, 82
  property of God, 44–46
prophets, 124,000, 34–35, 66

qabūl (accepted), 97
qadā' and qadar (decree and decreed), 94–95, 100–101
qalb (innermost heart), 85–90 *passim*, 100–101
  clear your, 82–83
  Light imprinted in your, 15–22 *passim*
  make the—of insān pure, 23–24
  of the Rasūl ☺ is squeezed, 5

qalb (continued)
  wash your, 41
  worship God within your, 27–29, 42–46 *passim*
qualities
  evil, 59, 61
  good, 61
Qur'ān, 30–31, 87–90
  inner meaning of the, 15–21 *passim*, 96–100 *passim*
  is revealed, 1–5
  Sharīf, 24, 28–49 *passim*
qurbān (sacrifice), 99
Qutb ☺ (the wondrous embodiment of īmān) know the, 5–6, 12–14, 20
Qutbiyyah (the state of the Qutb ☺), 28

Rabb (Lord), 'abd to the, 13–14
rahmah (compassionate grace), 11–21 *passim*, 94–95
Ramadān, 24, 51–57
Rasūl ☺, 24–25, 34, 45
  Qur'ān given to the, 2–6 *passim*
  See also Muhammad ☺
ray of Light, 24–28, 69–71, 74
representatives of God, 34–35
resplendences of grace, 69
reward of God, 71–74 *passim*, 83–84,
  seeking, 98
rich, man has become, 67
rocks, black—crushed, 16, 18, 22
rūh (soul), sent into man, 71

sadaqah (charity), give, 46
secrets within man, 102
shaitān (satan), 59, 61

smells, offensive, 40
soul
  doctor for the, 36
  sent into man, 71
sound(s)
  must come to the *qalb*, 96–97
  that came down on hajj, 78–79
speech without speech, 73
states, realize these, 30, 49
steps, God takes nine—towards man, 45
storybook, the Qur'ān without understanding is a, 30–31
sūrah(s) (chapter(s))
  first—given, 18
  revealed, 1–6 *passim*
Sūratul-Fātihah (the opening chapter of the Qur'ān), 7–8, 22
Sūratul-Ikhlas (Chapter of Sincerity), 8

tarāwih (prayers performed during Ramadān), 83–84
tasbīh (recitations glorifying God)
  everything does—to Allāh, 3
  perform—as a child in the womb, 25-28 *passim*
  perform—today, 39-42 *passim*, 45
tauhīd (the indivisible and absolute Oneness of God), 30
Tiru Maray (the Divine Qur'ān), 17
today, man has only, 39
toluhay (prayer, five-times prayer), 73
tomorrow is God's day, 38–39
treasures of God, 65, 72–73
trees, fruit on, 53

ummah (followers). See Muhammad ☮, *ummah* of
Ummul-Qur'ān (mother of the Qur'ān), 96–97

vanakkam (worship, prayer) 73–74

water, washing with, 40–42
wealth
  Allāh gives, 9
  of God, 63-65, 71, 75
  God protects our, 36
wilāyāt (the duties of God), 69
wisdom
  eye of, 100
  seven levels of, 87
  six levels of, 98
woman is God's *rahmah*, 43–44
work, selfish—of man, 64–75 *passim*
world is a museum, 97–98
worship
  God within your *qalb*, 27-29, 42-46 *passim*
  teaching your children how to, 78
wudū' (ablution), 47-48
  in sixteen steps, 40–42

young, become, 102

Zam-Zam, well of, 3–4, 86-87
zodiac, twelve houses of the, 98

A'ūdhu billāhi minash-shaitānir-rajīm.
I seek refuge in God from the accursed satan.

Bismillāhir-Rahmānir-Rahīm.
In the name of God, the Most Compassionate, the Most Merciful.

Muhammad Raheem Bawa Muhaiyaddeen ☙

The words of Muhammad Raheem Bawa Muhaiyaddeen ☙ reveal the Sufi path of esoteric Islām: that the human being is uniquely created with the faculty of wisdom, enabling him to trace himself back to his Origin—Allāh, the Creator and Cherisher of all the universes who exists in Oneness with all lives—and to surrender to that Source, leaving the One God, the Truth, as the only reality in his life. This is the original intention of the purity that is Islām.

Bawa Muhaiyaddeen ☙ spoke endlessly of this Truth through parables, discourses, songs, and stories, all pointing the way to return to God. Over fifteen thousand hours of this ocean of knowledge were recorded.

People of all ages, religions, classes, backgrounds, and races flocked to hear and be near him; he interacted compassionately and lovingly with all of them, opening his heart to them equally, regardless of who they were. Presidents of countries and fakirs from the streets, the proud and the humble, the high-ranking and the low-ranking, the ordinary and the extraordinary, the extremely poor and the extremely rich all sat side by side in his presence.

An extraordinary being, Bawa Muhaiyaddeen ☙ taught from experience, having traversed the path and returned, divinely aware—sent back to exhort all who yearn for the experience of God to discover the inner wisdom that is the path of surrender to that One.

Bawa Muhaiyaddeen ☙ did not tell us much about his life, although there were rare moments when he spoke to those gathered around him of certain memories.

What we know is that he was first sighted by spiritual

seekers—a man we know only as Periari and a few others from the town of Kokuvil—at the edge of the jungle near the pilgrimage town of Kataragama in what was then known as the island country of Ceylon.

The tiny island that is shaped like a teardrop falling from the tip of southern India is a place known for its legendary as well as its sacred geography. Adam's Peak in the center of the island is said to have retained the imprint created by the impact of Adam's foot from when he first touched the earth after being cast out of the Garden of Eden.

Referred to in the ancient text of the *Ramayana* as Lanka, it was the site of Princess Sita's captivity by her abductor, Ravana, the evil demon-king of Lanka. The *Ramayana* contains details of the battlefields where the armies of her husband Prince Rama fought the armies of the demon-king, and describes the groves of exotic herbs dropped by Hanuman, the monkey-king who helped Prince Rama rescue his wife.

When the island was called the Isle of Serendib, the voyage of Sinbad was described in *The Thousand and One Nights*. Medieval Arabs and Persians made regular pilgrimages to Adam's Peak. The fourteenth century Arab traveler and scholar Ibn Batutah made that pilgrimage.

Legends record the visit of the Qutb☻ who after visiting Adam's Peak meditated for twelve years in what came to be known as the hermitage shrine of Daftar Jailani that lies at the edge of a precipitous granite cliff in the south central portion of the island, a site that has become a place of saintly visitation and mystical meditation.

Living in that land of legends, those seekers from Kokuvil recognized Bawa Muhaiyaddeen☻ as a uniquely mystical being when they began to interact with him, begging him to teach them. He had lived peacefully alone in the jungle for so long that he had almost forgotten human speech. Gradually, he began to speak with those seekers.

Telling those seekers that God was the only Teacher, he

consented only to study side by side with them. Working long hours in the rice fields as a farmer by day, he spoke and sang to them of his experiences of God in the evenings. Eventually, he and that small group of seekers from Kokuvil built an ashram in Jaffna, a town in the northern tip of the country.

Travel was difficult in that small country, yet the refuge of his presence was irresistible. As more and more people came to know about him and to hear him sing and speak of God, many of them began to invite him to stay in their homes. Among those people were Dr. Ajwad Macan-Markar and his wife Ameen Macan-Markar who lived in the city of Colombo. Bawa Muhaiyaddeen ☺ told them it would not be easy: that he was like a tree upon which many birds needed to take shelter. If he was to agree to stay at their home, they would also have to accommodate these birds. He warned them that there could be many at times. Dr. Ajwad and his wife did not hesitate to agree to open their home to all who wished to accompany him. After that, Bawa Muhaiyaddeen ☺ always stayed at their home when he was in Colombo. For forty years Bawa Muhaiyaddeen ☺ spent his time with those seekers, until 1971.

In *The Tree That Fell to the West*,[1] Bawa Muhaiyaddeen ☺ tells us:

> "Before I arrived at 46th Street in Philadelphia for my first visit, Bob Demby, Carolyn Secretary, Zoharah Simmons and some others sitting here arranged for me to come.
>
> "They formed a society for that purpose, to invite me here. I did not come to Philadelphia with the idea of establishing a fellowship. There is only one Fellowship and that is Allāh's. There is only one family and one Fellowship. We are all the children of Adam ☺, and Allāh is in charge of that Fellowship."

---

1. Muhaiyaddeen, Bawa. *The Tree That Fell to the West.* Philadelphia: Fellowship Press, 2003. Print.

After that first visit, Bawa Muhaiyaddeen☺ went back and forth between Philadelphia and what by then had been renamed Sri Lanka until 1982, when he stayed in the United States until December 1986.

In these distressing times, his words are increasingly recognized as representing the original intention of Islām which is the purity of the relationship between man and God as explained by all the prophets of God, from Adam, Noah, Abraham, Ishmael, Moses, David, Jesus, and Muhammad, may the peace of God be upon them, who were all sent to tell and retell mankind that there is one and only One God, and that this One is their Source—attainable, and waiting for the return of each individual soul.

Publications

Books

Lailatul-Qadr: the Day of Light
Shaikh and Disciple
Islam, Jerusalem, and World Peace: Explanations of a Sufi
website: islamjerusalemandworldpeace.org
Prayer
Al-Asmā'ul Husnā: The Duties and Qualities of Allāh
website: asmaulhusna.org
The Choice
Bawa Asks Bawa Muhaiyaddeen ☺ (Volumes One, Two & Three)
Life Is a Dream: A Book of Sufi Verse
A Timeless Treasury of Sufi Quotations
The Four Virtues and Their Relationship
to Good Behavior and Bad Conduct
Sūratur-Rahmah: The Form of Compassion
God's Psychology: A Sufi Explanation
The Point Where God and Man Meet
The Map of the Journey to God: Lessons from the School of Grace
The Golden Words of a Sufi Sheikh, Revised Edition
A Book of God's Love
The Resonance of Allah: Resplendent Explanations Arising from
the Nūr, Allāh's Wisdom of Grace
The Tree That Fell to the West: Autobiography of a Sufi
Questions of Life — Answers of Wisdom (Volumes One & Two)
The Fast of Ramadan: The Inner Heart Blossoms
Hajj: The Inner Pilgrimage
The Triple Flame: The Inner Secrets of Sufism
A Song of Muhammad ☺
To Die Before Death: The Sufi Way of Life
A Mystical Journey
Sheikh and Disciple
Why Can't I See the Angels: Children's Questions to a Sufi Saint
Treasures of the Heart: Sufi Stories for Young Children
Come to the Secret Garden: Sufi Tales of Wisdom
My Love You My Children: 101 Stories for Children of All Ages
Maya Veeram or The Forces of Illusion
God, His Prophets and His Children
Four Steps to Pure *Īmān*

The Wisdom of Man
Truth & Light: Brief Explanations
Songs of God's Grace
The Guidebook to the True Secret of the Heart (Volumes One & Two)
The Divine Luminous Wisdom That Dispels the Darkness
Wisdom of the Divine (Volumes One to Six)
The Tasty, Economical Cookbook, Second Edition

BOOKLETS
Beyond Creation
Can We Ever Regain Our Innocence?
Come to Prayer: The Wake-up Song
Du'ā' Kanzul-'arsh (The Invocation of the Treasure of the Throne)
An Explanation of the Benefits of Reciting the *Salawāt*
The Foot of the Qutb ☉
The Hospital Story
King Solomon ☉ and the Fish & Explanations about Jinns and Fairies
The Opening of the Mosque of Shaikh M. R. Bawa Muhaiyaddeen ☉
Sindanay & I Will Tell You of the Way
Sufism
Why We Recite the Maulids

A CONTEMPORARY SUFI SPEAKS SERIES
On the Meaning of Fellowship
Mind, Desire, and the Billboards of the World
On Peace of Mind
On the Signs of Destruction
Teenagers and Parents
On the True Meaning of Sufism
On Unity: The Legacy of the Prophets
Gems of Wisdom series:
Vol. 1: The Value of Good Qualities
Vol. 2: Beyond Mind and Desire
Vol. 3: The Innermost Heart
Vol. 4: Come to Prayer

THE INSTRUCTIONS
The Fox and the Crocodile and Do Not Carry Tales
God Is Very Light
Prayer: Starting Over
Unity

PAMPHLETS

Advice to Prisoners
Faith
The Golden Words of a Sufi Sheikh: Preface to the Book
Grieving for the Dead
Keep the Pond Clean
Letter to the World Family
Love Is the Remedy, God Is the Healer
Marriage
A Prayer for Father's Day
A Prayer for My Children
A Prayer from My Heart
Strive for a Good Life
Sufi: A Brief Explanation
A Sufi Perspective on Business
25 Duties – The True Meaning of Fellowship
Who Is God?
With Every Breath, Say Lā Ilāha Ill-Allāhu
Why Man Has No Peace (from My Love You, My Children)
The Wisdom and Grace of the Sufis

FOREIGN LANGUAGE PUBLICATIONS

Ein Zeitgenössischer Sufi Spricht über Inneren Frieden
Deux Discours tirés du Livre L'Islam et la Paix Mondiale:
Explications d'un Soufi
La Paix
Quién es Dios? Una Explicatión por el Sheikh Sufi

OTHER PUBLICATIONS

Bawa Muhaiyaddeen Fellowship Calendar
Morning *Dhikr*
at the Mosque of Shaikh M. R. Bawa Muhaiyaddeen ☺
Songs of Divine Wisdom
(a notated version of songs by M. R. Bawa Muhaiyaddeen ☺
The *Subhāna Maulid*

WE INVITE YOU TO VISIT

The Fellowship in Philadelphia, Pennsylvania, where Bawa Muhaiyaddeen ☙ stayed when he visited the United States, continues to serve as a meeting house and a reservoir of materials for everyone wishing access to his teachings.

The Mosque of Shaikh M. R. Bawa Muhaiyaddeen ☙ is located on the same property as the Fellowship. The five daily prayers and Friday congregational prayers are observed.

The Mazār, the resting place of Bawa Muhaiyaddeen ☙, is an hour west of the Fellowship and open daily between sunrise and sunset.

email: **info@bmf.org**
website: **www.bmf.org/publications**

TO LISTEN TO THE TEACHINGS

http://s3.nexuscast.com/start/bmfdd/
The Daily Discourse: the teachings of Bawa Muhaiyaddeen ☙ in chronological order, beginning every even hour on the hour, Eastern Time [GMT-5].

http://sc1.mystreamserver.com/start/bmfhs/
Live from the Fellowship House and Mosque: morning *dhikr*, five-times prayer, Bawa Muhaiyaddeen's discourses and songs, meetings, and special events.

http://s3.nexuscast.com/start/bmf786/
24/7 Radio: a continuous stream of over 300 discourses and songs from the CD of the Month, updated every Anniversary Weekend.

Al-hamdu lillāh, all praise is due to God!

www.ingramcontent.com/pod-product-compliance
Lightning Source LLC
Chambersburg PA
CBHW071510150426
43191CB00009B/1469